INSANE RAIN

A Life Saved and Directed by Spiritual and Psychical Events

Art Seter

ISBN 979-8-88644-362-2 (Paperback)
ISBN 979-8-88644-363-9 (Digital)

Covenant Books
11661 Hwy 707
Murrells Inlet, SC 29576
www.covenantbooks.com

Acknowledgments

When weird events happened in my life, it was a relief to know that similar things had happened to my mom and siblings during my childhood, although I believe some would not talk about them thinking they may be thought to be insane. Later when my son Chad saw the same weird events I saw, it further verified I was not hallucinating or imagining them. I thank my family for supporting my writing of this book and encouraging me to get it published.

I thank my sister Margaret for sharing her experience, reading the first unedited manuscript, suggesting removing some ridiculous attempts at adding humor, and finding several errors. Since I never learned to type, I use what someone once called "the Columbus method, discover a key and land on it," so there were many errors because my fingers often land on the wrong key or more than one key at a time.

Thanks to my sister Marcia and my niece Debbie for helping bolster my belief that we have lived previous lives and have spirit friends we communicate with when we are very young. Part of the proof for me that spirit friends exist is that I doubt an imaginary friend could be imagined to say something so sad that it would make you cry.

To my daughter Phyllis (who also read and commented on the unedited manuscript) and my granddaughter Mina, you strengthened my belief that our departed relatives' spirits are often near us shortly after death and even years after they passed from this life. Thank you again for encouraging me to get this published.

Thank you, Betty (my sister-in-law), for keeping old photographs from Grandma's farm and providing scanned copies of them on CD to members of our family.

Last but not least, thank you, Kasha Foret, Sandra Jarvis, and the editors at Covenant Books for accepting my manuscript for publication and for your efforts to make it into a readable book.

Introduction

I wrote this book because my life did, at times, seems to border on the insane, sometimes fun, sometimes sad, disgusting, interesting, and so many adjectives I can't even think of to describe my time on earth up to now. It took me until this late in life to write a book because I guess I was waiting for something spectacular to write about, and also, I never knew when something important was going to occur that I could include. It turned out something did happen in September 2020. Or maybe I was just too lazy to do it earlier.

Everything in this book actually happened as I describe it. Nothing is exaggerated or described any different from how it occurred even if it was boring the way it was.

I pose many questions about my life, some of which I will present some theories on possible answers to, maybe being absurd or maybe right on. Nowhere else did I find any really good explanations for the experiences I had. Some of the questions I had about things that happened in my life are as follows.

How did we survive life on our farm? (I may not have an answer for that.)

How did Mom know exactly how, but not when, she would die? How did she know one of my many brothers was in a position that could end his life and tell another brother where he was and to go rescue him? Why and how did I clearly hear her call my name years after she passed away?

How did I and others in the family experience events several minutes before they actually happened?

How did I unconsciously go out of my way to avoid what could have been nasty or dangerous events and actually saved my own life? In other words, why am I still alive?

How do I perceive spirits being around at times even though I don't see them, but sometimes I did?

How did I dream future events?

How was my daughter able to talk to my dad even though he had been dead for several months?

How is our UNIVERSE constructed and how does that help explain why things happen as they do? I have some explanations which may or may not be insane.

There are some more, but that should do for now. You just have to read the rest of this book to see that some weird things happen to some of us. As I said, I will try to explain how some of this could happen actually using some science, maybe a little pseudoscience and a form of theology to explain it.

I will start my book probably boring you to death describing life and working on our grandma's farm. I think you will find it— well, maybe pathetic. Hopefully, you will find some of it interesting.

1

Existing on Grandma's Farm

Life is supposed to be fun sometimes, but maybe "living" on the farm is a stretch. But in any case, I was born and grew up on a farm in north-central North Dakota. If I had been born five miles farther north, I would have been a Canadian. I was a bit less than two years old when Japan attacked Pearl Harbor, so I lived through all of the officially active U.S. part of WWII.

I was one of thirteen kids that lived to be adults. I was number eleven of the thirteen crowd and I had a little younger brother named Paul who died at almost eighteen months old shortly before I turned three. I was told he was a fighter, kind of mean to me, and was tougher than I was. I don't remember him at all except the pictures I've seen.

If we had all lived, there would have been seventeen of us. There were eight boys and five girls who grew up to be adults. We were, in order of birth: Marvin, Howard (John), Gretchen, Lester (Vernon), Luella (Vivian) and Lynn (a boy) who were twins, Clair (another boy), Gordon, Shirley, Calvin, me (Art), Marcia, and Margaret. Whenever Mom (we actually called Mom and Dad Ma and Pa) called me by my nickname, which was just as long as my real name, she would pronounce it like two words *art-tea* (the first part would have been enough), and everyone else used Artie. Even my nieces and nephews picked that up.

We also called each other some very strange names, but I won't reveal any of those! I guess this was just one of the things we did for entertainment because when you live in North Dakota during the winter, you have to have a good or maybe weird sense of humor! One of my brothers gave me a nickname that had somewhere around sixty-nine letters depending on how you spelled it! I still remember the whole thing; and one time, several years ago, when I wrote him and his wife a letter, I signed it that way. His wife said it really cracked him up because he had forgotten it until then, but that as she read it, he joined in to finish the rest of it. I did comment that with a nickname like that, maybe you didn't spell it; you smelled it.

Life on the farm was really hard, but I am glad I went through that experience because I can really appreciate what I have now. I always say North Dakota is a great place to be *from*. I couldn't move back there for anything (well most anything). I probably couldn't survive the winters there now at my age. But I do miss some of what we had: northern lights are pretty, snow can be beautiful, spring is always great, fall colors are spectacular, but -20 to -50 degrees temperature (we had those numbers) in winter is numbing.

Minnesota has "10,000 Lakes" on their license plates; North Dakota could have had "A Billion Ponds," but we had Peace Garden State named after the Peace Garden, which straddles the border of North Dakota and Manitoba, Canada, instead. Seriously, if you ever drive or have driven North Dakota highways, you go over these low rolling hills; and in each low spot in the ditches or the farmer's fields along the highway, there is a tiny lake, each a breeding area for mosquitos.

There were millions of mosquitos in the spring through fall evenings when the weather was cool, and in the summer and early fall, millions of other flying and jumping bugs were airborne and you couldn't drive ten miles without accumulating a windshield full of bug guts and wings. It is still a great place though. I can't imagine how some motorcyclists without windshields did what they did! They must have loved the wind in their hair and the taste of bugs.

The farmland had been developed by my grandpa John who had changed his name at some time to Seter, which I believe in Norwegian means mountain meadow or pasture. It is not the name of the Setter dog misspelled, but it is pronounced the same. If he hadn't changed it, I would have been a Halverson. Some say he changed it after he got Grandma pregnant and flew the coop to avoid getting hitched and that great-grandpa chased him across country for a shotgun wedding, but I can't be sure of that.

I do know that it was only a couple months between their marriage and the birth of my dad. I believe that Grandma hated Dad for that reason, which is totally unreasonable because his existence wasn't his fault. I guess we can draw our own conclusions from the dates. Both Mom and Dad's sides of the family were supposedly pure Norwegian, whatever that really means; therefore, I guess my siblings and I must be too. Norwegian ancestry is really hard to trace back very far because of the way they named the kids, so my ancestry is a bit hazy more than about three generations back. But both sides of the family came from Norway.

I was quite a daredevil when I was young, but I don't remember now what caused Mom's comment. Was it when I tried to fly by jumping off the barn roof (it was fairly low in places) holding a board above my head like a wing? It didn't work! I landed quite hard, and the board then hit me on my head. That hurt for quite a while. Maybe it was the time I was trying to tease a young bull with one of Dad's red handkerchiefs. Luckily, the bull ignored me.

Her comment is why I chose the name for this book. She said, "Insanity reigns where you are!" Of course, not understanding the different word meanings at the time, I had the impression of insane rain coming out of the sky. Not sure what insanity would look like falling out of the sky, but it would probably be pretty interesting and maybe quite scary. Pretty sure she said that more than once too. My interpretation is similar to a joke I once heard about a little kid being exposed to church services for the first time. He said that the minister said, "Everyone would be burning in hell forever if they didn't repent, whatever that meant." And was mean and insulting because he said, "we are all butt dust." I will be writing about a lot of "insane rain" in future chapters because I went through a lot of it.

The farm, which was then owned by Dad's mother, was a square mile in size, minus approximately eighty acres in the southeast corner where the original log cabin Turtle Mountain Church had been built and that land had been sold to our neighbor Eddy when the church got built a few miles southwest of that location. The farm was located about three-quarters of a mile from the foothills of the Turtle Mountains, which are really just hills. There were gravel roads on all four sides of it until the main road on the west side (State Highway 14) was paved in about the 1970s.

SR-14 led north into Canada and south through the mighty city of Carbury (population thirty-five or maybe even up to fifty when I was very young). None of the county roads were named then, making it really hard to describe where a family lived since no one had a street or road address. The city (village on the map) of Carbury consisted of a blacksmith shop, a post office (in a home), and train depot and telegraph office, three grain elevators, a school, the telephone office (in a home), a meeting hall, a grocery store (which I don't remember), and maybe about ten to twelve homes.

The streets of Carbury were gravel or dirt with grass in the middle, and there were no sidewalks, just ditches along the streets. The town had electricity but no running water unless people put it into their homes from a well (which some did). I know at least one had a well and a septic tank for sewage and I suspect others did too, but there were several outdoor toilets decorating the town.

The farmhouse was three-and-a-half miles from Carbury and about four miles from Canada. The farm was one of many in the area at that time. I remember seeing and hearing a steam train puffing through Carbury every day with billowing gray clouds of smoke and steam. Later (maybe early fifties), the engines were replaced with diesel ones, which were not as exciting but sounded very powerful and put out black smoke when they accelerated.

With the wide-open spaces in North Dakota, sound seemed to travel forever, and you could hear them both really well. Trains don't run there anymore. There are fewer farms buildings around the area, and all the farm buildings are gone from Grandma's old farm where I lived. Traveling there a few years ago, I still could see the small mound of dirt where the barn and manure pile were when I lived there though!

When I lived there, we had a house (of course), barn, a granary with a large (a sort of lean-to) garage for farm machinery, another granary, a chicken coop, and a brooder house for raising chicks, outdoor toilet, and a pigpen with a small covered enclosure. The garage contained a big coal bin, fuel tanks and oil tanks for the tractor and other powered equipment, the tractor, grain planter, disk, tiller, and harrow. The large equipment like the grain binder and threshing machine (later the combine) were outside all the time. The three-bottom plow stayed outside, and we kept the plow shares covered with grease to keep them from rusting. The granary part had a couple of grain bins and an upstairs room containing tools and a large foot-pedal-operated knife and axe sharpener. The farm buildings were located about one-eighth of a mile from the northeast corner of the property.

There were large trees consisting of box elder, elm, and cottonwood to the north, north-east, and south of the main buildings. Cottonwoods had little cottony covered seeds that blew a long distance in the wind. The box elder had little half propellers for seeds that would spin as they fell, and they were fun to toss in the air and watch them spin coming down. The elm had little bulges on the leaf stem that had little bugs living in them quite often. A large lilac bush along with some other bushes grew on the east side of the house and, when it bloomed, smelled great.

There were some hollyhocks, wild roses, a berry bush (currents), and rhubarb growing in the area. There were pin cherries, gooseberries, a crab apple, and a plum tree in the trees to the south of the house that produced tasty fruit in the fall. The pin cherries, gooseberries, and crab apples caused your mouth to pucker a bit but had great flavor. Maybe I just couldn't wait till they were ripe! There was one large tree that had a branch, maybe about six to eight inches thick, that grew bent near the bottom of the tree and was parallel with the ground for maybe six or seven feet. The branch was about four feet off the ground.

It was fun to get up on the branch and bounce up and down like riding a horse, unless someone else pushed it up and down real fast and you (if you were a boy) crushed something! Then it would hurt a lot! At the west end of the trees south of the house was a small patch of rhubarb and wild parsnips, and between that area and building with the garage grew three to four-foot-tall thin bushes we called burning grass. It you touched the leaves, your skin would burn and itch, and if you scratched, it would form a rash. If you didn't scratch and washed it off, it would quit burning and itching sooner. We also had poison ivy in a pasture in the hills, but as a kid, it never bothered me and I never bothered it either.

I was told the house had started out as a log cabin and part of the cabin still existed in some of the walls, but I don't remember which part or whether the log cabin had just been replaced by a new part of the house. The two-story house had ten rooms: kitchen, dining room, pantry, parlor (well that's what we called it), Mom and Dad's bedroom downstairs, and five bedrooms upstairs. But one of them was really a hallway that contained beds. There were some holes here and there along the baseboards where mice had been at work. We had mice in the house to make noise in the walls at night so it wouldn't be too darn quiet! There were no other sounds around there at night except for crickets, frogs, and the occasional hoot of an owl or the sound of coyotes and wolves in the hills.

In the kitchen, located at the southeast corner of the house, were a couch, a table and chairs and a second cook stove (the one used the most was in the dining room) and there was a square hole in the floor with a lift-off lid. It covered a concrete-lined cistern that filled with water from the gutters on the house when it rained. I don't remember what happened when it rained more than it would hold, and it seemed to have a lot of water in it most of the time. I am not sure whether there was an overflow on it.

The water was used for washing clothes or bathing. It was the only source of soft water we had. It was cool in the cistern, and we kept milk and cream in sealed jars in a bucket hooked to a rope in there that we would pull out when needed. We kept stuff cool that way until we got a gas-operated refrigerator. It was really neat to have ice in the summer after we got the refrigerator, although you could find ice around the trees under leaves and stuff if it had been a long winter with lots of snow well into June. One time, I remember finding some in July among the trees north of the house.

We would use the ice we found along with some salt to make ice cream in an ice cream freezer. The kitchen had a view out the window on the east side; and in winter, when the trees had no leaves, you could see the moon rising and illuminating the snow. Many times, there would be a herd of deer coming out of the hills. It was great.

We kept our washing machine in the kitchen during the winter and moved it outside on the porch or even in the yard in the summer. The washing machine was a gasoline-powered Maytag that had a wringer for squeezing the water out of the clothes. When I was between twelve and seventeen, the washing machine motor was getting old and needed overhauling very often when we were going to wash; so I had to take it apart, clean the carburetor, and adjust it before it would start. The clothes were dried on a clothesline outside unless the weather was way too bad and then it was put on a wooden drying rack that unfolded to look like a tent when it was covered with clothes.

It was funny in the winter when clothes were hung on the line outside to dry in the sun, they would freeze stiff and you could hold a pair of pants straight out by one leg or walk around holding a shirt; and your shadow looked like you were with a legless, headless, person with handless arms in the air! They would eventually dry out there, but it took time. The soap Mom used for washing clothes was home-made lye soap. Mom made it by boiling fat from animals we had butchered mixed with lye that would break down the fat, and then make it into big bricks of yucky-looking and smelling brown soap.

She would take a knife and peel off thin slices whenever she washed clothes and dissolve them in the washing machine. For a hot water wash, she had to heat the water on the cook stove. Sometimes, Mom or an older sister would use the old rubbing board for washing clothes, and there was a hand-operated portable ringer that could be attached to the side of a big tub. They were used quite a bit.

The dining room had a cook stove, wood box, coal bucket, a large table, chairs, china cabinet, and the only telephone in the house. The telephone, mounted on the wall, had a crank on the right side, a mouthpiece on the front, and an earphone on a wire on a cradle on the left side of the phone. We had a party line, and we heard every time anyone on the party line got a call. To make a call, you pick up the earphone which turned on the phone and crank the proper ring code of the party you were calling.

Our call was a long, a short, and two long rings. Mom would get all the gossip by listening to calls between other people, which was called rubbernecking. The same word applies to people who slow down and watch accidents on the highway, so maybe it originated in stretching the neck or swiveling the head to look at stuff happening like your neck was made of rubber or something. Maybe that is why I don't talk a whole lot. I was always being shushed when she was rubbernecking, which seemed to be every time I wanted to tell her something!

To make a call outside your party line, you would pick up the earphone, call the operator by turning the crank one long ring, tell her whom you wanted to call, and she would connect two sockets with a cable on the switchboard to the party line you were calling. To make the call, she would crank in the proper code (rings) for that family on the other party line. She would then wait to see if they answered and probably listened if the gossip was juicy. After the call, she would simply pull out the cable. If you were calling long distance, she would connect you to the operator in another town. I suspect out-of-state calls required several operators.

The pantry was located off the dining room and had shelves all around the walls where we kept some mixing bowls, stuff to cook with, and much of the canned goods. There was a hole in the floor to basically a hole in the ground (the cellar) where it was cool, and we stored potatoes and some other vegetables and had some more shelves for canned stuff. It was musty down there, and there were always spiders and bugs. The hole had a lift-off lid like the cistern, but this hole had a vertical ladder inside and there was a window in the foundation of the house that let in a little light.

Dad had later started digging out a basement under the pantry and dining room and had it about half-finished when we left the farm in 1957. He had some of the basement walls up, and there were jacks in places under the floor of the house holding it up until he could get the basement walls and other supports completed, which never happened.

There was a cream separator in the pantry with a large tank on top with a valve on it to control the flow of milk into the separator cylinder. It had two spouts. Milk came out the bottom one and cream out the top one. We had to crank the thing fairly hard and steady to make it work. We would take some of the cream into town (Bottineau) to the creamery in an eight-gallon cream can and sell it.

The man at the creamery was a big man, probably because he would stick his finger in the cream and taste it to see if it was sweat or sour. If he did that for every can delivered, he must have eaten a lot of cream each day. The building where we took the cream had a potbelly stove for heat in the winter. Some of the cream we would keep and churn to make butter in the hand-operated butter churn made out of wood that had a horizontal cylinder shape about sixteen inches in diameter, had an opening with lid on top, and a wooden paddle wheel inside that you cranked on the end with a metal crank. The crank had a square shaft with round bearing surfaces on both ends that fit through the paddle wheel, and there was a clip-type device and wing nut to hold the shaft in place.

It was fairly easy to turn until the cream thickened and butter separated from the buttermilk. Then, the butter would tend to bind the paddle and it would get hard to turn. It was good exercise. We used the buttermilk to make pancakes and waffles or to drink. In the pantry, we kept another eight-gallon cream can that we used for drinking water that we hauled from the well. It was quite heavy when it was full but manageable if you used both hands or were as strong as a gorilla!

Sometimes, we hauled the water in buckets to fill the can that way. The water buckets and cream cans would slowly rust and get holes in them, and we soldered the holes with lead solder or use little special bolts with gaskets called Mend-its (or something like that).

Before the little repair devices were available, we probably got a little bit of lead from the soldered buckets as well as from any painting we did with lead-based paint, but we all seemed to be okay.

We had a five-gallon bucket we used for a slop bucket in the pantry. All the food that no one could eat, coffee grounds, fruit and vegetable peelings, corn husks, carrot tops, all things rotten, fat from the meat, chicken innards, anything biodegradable, dishwater, and sometimes eggshells went into the five-gallon slop bucket. In summer, when it was hot, this thing got quite aromatic before we hauled it out.

Each day, we hauled the slop bucket, hopefully without spilling all over ourselves or the floor, about seventy-five yards to the pigpen; and the pigs would have a feast. The pigs usually got whole or ground barley and oats and water with the slop all together in a big feeding trough. That stuff must have been heavenly to the pigs, but it smelled a lot like the other place! The pigpen was very aromatic also. I understand that slop bucket was instrumental in putting out a fire one night when I, a very young child at the time, wanted a drink of water and woke up sister Shirley to get it for me.

There was a fire in the pantry. A mouse had chewed into a cardboard box of wooden matches that were on the pantry shelf. I don't remember whether I ever got the drink of water. The pantry must have been fun to clean up after that. I have no idea about the condition of the mouse, but he must have fried his nose real fast when the matches all flared up. It was nowhere to be found and must have survived to get away at least for a little while. I think Dad set some traps, and we kept the matches in a metal container after that.

In our parlor, we had a large leather couch, which turned into a bed, a big cozy chair, a rocking chair, and a big furnace that burned wood and coal. There was no heat ducting to other rooms in the house on the furnace, and it was hottest close to it than anywhere else in the house in the winter. Mom had two pianos, a dresser, a china closet, a cedar chest, and a couple of tables with flowers and cactus plants.

We had an AM radio powered by a battery that was about four-by-six-by-sixteen inches or maybe three by five by twelve (everything looked bigger when you were a kid) and had the high voltage for the vacuum tube plate supply, a low-voltage negative voltage for the vacuum tube grid supply, and a low-voltage high current for the vacuum tube cathode heaters (wow things are simple now). Those vacuum tubes, made of glass, were about the size of a small cell phone. There were several types with different arrangements of anodes, cathodes, and grids to process the signal; and the radio needed several of them, each having a specialized job.

We would turn the radio on, it would warm up, and about a minute or two later, we're receiving the signal. It seemed like the battery was always dying and having to be replaced. Dad liked to listen to the newscasters Gabriel Heatter, Edward R Murrow, and of course one I even liked to listen to, Paul Harvey. I liked to listen to *X-One* (a sci-fi program), and Mom listened to her soap operas like *Fibber McGee* and *Molly* (Fibber McGee's closet unloaded itself accompanied by bangs, clatters, and shatters when he opened the door), which started out as a comedy but turned into a very serious soap opera.

It was a fun program at first, I thought, but became pathetic as a soap opera. A few other programs I remember were *Sky King, Red Skelton, Superman, Sgt. Preston of the Yukon, The Shadow, Green Hornet, Amos and Andy, Lone Ranger, Boston Blackie, Jack Benny, Edgar Bergen*, and *George Burns and Gracie Allan*. Vivian told me there was a program called *The Evening Mystery Theater* and another called *I Love a Mystery*, but I don't remember those shows.

Edgar Bergen was a ventriloquist, and now that seems really strange to have listened to him on the radio. It loses something in the translation! The radio had a wire that was strung between the house and the trees on the north side of the house for an antenna. I can't really knock radio because it made you think and visualize things you heard, and sometimes that would be funnier or more exciting than actually seeing it happen, like Fibber McGee's closet for instance.

We also heard Canadian radio stations, and I thought some of them talked funny, especially words like *schedule* which they pronounced *shed-yule*. Besides a few local stations, I remember one that we heard at night when I was a teenager that was fun to listen to. It was KOMA Oklahoma City, Oklahoma, and the station must have been required to change its antenna pattern at night and we got a good signal skipped off the ionosphere.

They played a lot of good music and had some pretty interesting DJs. We also had record players of various kinds that played 78 RPM records. Later versions had three speeds: 78, 45, and 33 RPM. There was one that operated at 16 RPM too, but I never saw a record that was recorded to run at that speed. We had to keep them wound up using a crank on the side or the music would slow down and sound a bit funny. One of those had a hornlike thing on it where the sound came out.

Upstairs were the four bedrooms and a hall that served as a bedroom, but later, one bedroom became a clothes room with clothes just kind of piled on the floor about two feet deep. There were shelves in the room that had boxes of pictures and so on. The bedroom in the northwest corner had had an upper porch deck that matched the porch downstairs at one time, but they were both gone as long back as I remember.

The door on the north side or back side of the house that used to go to the upper porch deck was still there, and it opened to what would now have been a very large down-only step (about ten to twelve feet) since the deck had been torn down. The one below that one was in the parlor, and it had a door that also opened to a big step down (maybe two-and-a-half feet). I don't think anyone ever made the mistake of using them.

Now that I think about it, I wonder why nobody thought to build steps for the parlor door so that it could be used. Mom and Dad's bedroom was off the living room on the northeast corner of the house. There was a table in there with plants on it too. There were no built-in closets in there, so they had a cabinet for their clothes. They weren't too far from the heater in the living room, so they slept a lot more comfortable in the winter than some who were upstairs. When it was very cold and there was no heat ducting, the three heat sources weren't very effective to heat much of the house.

My bedroom was the one with the down-only step farthest from the heat sources when I was a teenager, and I had a glass of water in the room freeze solid one winter night. In winter, we all had a lot of covers on the beds, so once I was in bed and had shivered to get warmed up, I didn't want to move again because some part of my body would find a cold spot! I couldn't have my head out from under the covers either, or I'd freeze something.

The windows were not real well sealed, so in the morning, I would find a small snowdrift on the top of the covers and in the room if there was a lot of snow blowing during the night. In the morning, I got dressed, shivering to get warm again because the clothes are cold or, as I did many times, put the clothes under the covers in bed until they warm up a little. They would make it colder in the bed for a while but were not as hard to put on then. In summer, the rooms never seemed to cool off until about early morning, and even sheets were too hot to sleep under.

The farm had no electricity and no running water. We had a well where we got our water about fifty or sixty yards from the barn and about the same distance from the house. I think it was seventy-five feet deep and had a wooden casing about three feet across and a platform on top with a large handled pump where we pumped our water for use in the house and water for the cattle in a large metal tank.

We pumped water by hand, except when we could get the various engines to work to operate a pump jack on the well and then the handle would be disconnected. I remember the engine that was the most fascinating was a hit-and-miss engine with two big flywheels. It would run with a *pop-pop-pop-pop* and then a *puff-puff-puff-puff* with the valves open, and when it slowed a little, it would fire again. Pictures exist of the farm with a windmill and a better-looking barn, but I don't remember seeing that farm configuration.

A tornado had destroyed some of the buildings and nothing was rebuilt the same, and much had changed from those pictures when I arrived on the scene. I remember seeing some tangled metal that used to be the windmill near a large stone pile when I went exploring on the farm, which I did quite frequently. There was lots of junk out there to play with or make something to play with.

Our lights consisted of kerosene lamps and lanterns with glass chimneys that had braided fabric wicks, and we had gas lanterns that burned a very pure and colorless form of gasoline. The gasoline lanterns had a built-in pump to pressurize the gas tank, a device that was heated to vaporize the gasoline and burned the vaporized gasoline in mantles that gave off a very white light.

The device for vaporizing the gasoline had to be replaced sometimes. The mantles being tied on were made of a very soft material that shrank and became flimsy ash with the first burning, but they gave off a lot of light almost like a light bulb. The mantles, being ashes in the form of a bulb, would fall apart easily when the lantern was bumped; and they had to be replaced often.

The cook stoves had flat iron tops with round lids and parts between the lids that could be removed to heat large pans over the fire, but we usually used only the round openings for cooking in pots unless we were cooking a lot of stuff at once then we put them on top of the lids. When you built a fire in the stoves, you would have to watch the fire and adjust the damper in the pipe to the chimney and/ or on the stove to keep the fire from getting too hot. If the stove got too hot, it could start a chimney fire. I remember a few times the top of the stove and part of the pipes to the chimney glowing cherry red when the fire was a bit too high.

The outhouse (toilet) was in the trees south of the house about a hundred feet from the house. That is a long way to go in the winter when you must go, and we had to make sure we took gloves along to sweep the snow off the seat before you sat down. It was a double wide outhouse with one small hole shaped like a skull and one large round one giving us our choice of seats, uncomfortable or extremely uncomfortable.

In winter, snow would blow in around the door and through any cracks in the walls and collect inside and on the seat. At times, the wind would blow the door open, and it got deep enough in there you had to shovel snow out before you could use it. Sometimes, the snow had melted and frozen, and we got to sit on ice or had to chip it off first. We used newspapers, Sears and Wards catalogs, and some magazines for a source of paper, not for reading; but I suppose if you planned to be there some time, you could read what was left!

It was frustrating to start reading an interesting article and find it wasn't all there. Reading the material was not much of a problem in the winter because we were in a big hurry to get our business done and get out of there. That outhouse made life very interesting sometimes! Mom and Dad also had a bucket (one of the five-gallon ones) in the bedroom that they used during the night and emptied the next day in the outhouse.

Marvin built a small seven- or eight-foot tower by the well, put a tank on top, and put plumbing in for a shower under the tower. In the summer we would fill it with water in the morning using a little gas engine and a pump, and by evening, it had warmed to lukewarm in the sun. It probably held a couple hundred gallons. There was a canvas curtain around under the platform. It worked well, and I am sure felt great after a day of hard work. I was a little guy at the time, so I didn't get to use it very many times. Eventually, it leaked or something and was taken down or maybe it blew over in the wind.

Howard owned the "mountain pasture" in the hills where we kept the cattle in the summer during the daytime between morning and evening milking. We also had a pasture on the farm, which was kind of *L* shaped south and east side of the main buildings, which I will call the south pasture. Both pastures had watering holes fed by springs for the cattle. Periodically, we would have to take the tractor and a big scoop to clean the mud out of one of the springs in the hills. This was not a whole lot of fun!

In the winter, the cows were kept in the barn. In the mountain pasture between the hills were three parallel ravines that were full of trees and bushes. There were oak, poplar, elm, and birch trees as well as plums, hazelnuts, currants, pin cherries, chokecherries, blueberries, raspberries, strawberries, black haws, and highbush cranberries scattered through the ravines and in an area on a flat part of the property on the corner nearest the farm. Little worms got most of the nuts, except for the acorns on the oak trees.

One thing that grew in profusion all over was a plant we called silver willow that grew about three to four feet tall and had a metallic-gray silvery colored leaf, and the whole plant was that color. There was also diamond willow growing in the southeastern corner of the pasture. It can be stripped of bark, polished, and varnished to make beautiful furniture, lamps, canes, or whatever. On the hills were wild onions and cactus berries that grew on little, almost-flat cactus about the size of half a baseball.

At certain times of the year, with all the fruit, berries, nuts, and these two little items, you could feast as you went to bring the cattle home for milking. Everyone within a half mile knew if you had eaten some wild onions! At the end of one of the ravines in the neighbor's property was an artesian well. The artesian well was interesting in the winter because it would create a mound of ice maybe a foot high that had an interesting layered shape. There was also quicksand in that area, so I didn't go out there except in winter when everything was frozen.

At the northeast corner of the farm where two county roads meet, there is a wagon/car trail going east to the gate to enter the pasture in the hills. The trail splits with one going to the gate and another that went east on the south side of the pasture fence. Between the two trails was a grove of trees maybe seventy-five feet long east and west by twenty feet wide with a dense growth of chokecherries, small oak trees, and some tall brush. The left trail went directly to the gate and the other maybe thirty feet away on the southeast side of the grove of trees. The right trail was used a lot to go into the woods to gather firewood on a property Dad owned in the hills about six to eight miles away.

In the pasture on the farm, there was quite a large stone pile, the one I mentioned earlier, with some huge stones that had been taken off the fields where the old car bodies, rusted farm equipment, wheels, tires, and gears were piled. There was part of an old Model T that had the three peddles on the floor. They operated transmission bands, and the transmission operated similar to some older automatic ones used today.

Someone told me once that they had cotton bands. People who did drive the Model T would also "ride the clutches" on the newer cars with the three-speed transmissions. But I am getting off the subject. This was a great place to play around when I was a kid. I would make a fort or a cave between the big rocks or whatever with the metal pieces, tires, and other junk. It is where the parts of the old windmill were too. There were always little critters like gophers and mice running around, and garter snakes were out there too. We didn't have any poisonous snakes in our area. There was a bunch of burning grass and a lot of silver willow growing near the stone pile. When I was a teenager, we hauled a lot of the junk into town and loaded it onto railcars after it had been weighed and got a few bucks for it.

Because I want to give you an idea of how life was on the farm, the boring stuff will continue in the next chapters; but I hope you will think there is exciting, weird, almost impossible, and interesting stuff after that. Our life was hard with lots of work every day, and my life got really weird at times. I never had time to get bored much, but sometimes I did. My life seemed to be guided in one direction or maybe misguided in one direction pretty much all the way until now.

As unbelievable as it sounds, everything in this book is true, and all the weird stuff happened to me exactly as I describe it. My memory of it is still very vivid; therefore, I have to get this done before creeping codgerhood and forgetfulness take over my life. I wonder what sort of weird stuff will still happen to me in the future, or maybe all the weird stuff already happened and there won't be any more. I am not psychic enough to know.

After I wrote this, another weird thing did happen that I write about in chapter 16.

2

Doing Chores and Other Things

In winter, we burned a lot of coal. It seemed to me it was always my job to bring in the coal from the garage/toolshed where it was stored. Like a dummy, I always procrastinated and then had to get it in the dark, carrying one of the lanterns. Now that I think about it, in midwinter, it got dark so early that after school, I didn't have time before it got dark.

Sometimes, I could con one of my younger sisters into carrying the lantern for me. I would haul the coal on our snow sled. We always were cleaning ashes from the stoves; and when you burned coal, it sometimes had seams of clay in the coal that, after it was burned, formed hard weird-shaped things called clinkers that were so named because they clinked when you hit them together or against anything.

We bought our coal near the train depot in Carbury where we loaded it straight from a freight car parked on a railroad siding. We sometimes got the lignite (soft coal), and I think it may have been the kind that contained the most clay that created the clinkers. At night in winter, we filled the stoves with coal and turned the damper to keep the fire way down low to make it burn slowly all night. In summer, the stoves still had to be used for cooking, but we would let them go out at night and burned wood when we needed to cook.

We milked the cows every morning and evening by hand. We sometimes gave them some hay or grain if they weren't busy chewing their cuds while we did the milking. Pull up a stool beside the cow, support a pail between your knees, and start squeezing one in each hand, alternating left and right. Keep that up until no more milk came out, then finish the other two and move to the next cow. Sometimes, a cat would show up, and it was fun to squirt milk at them and see how expertly they caught it in their mouths.

Usually, they had faces covered with milk, but they seemed to love it! We milked six to ten cows, the number depending on whether some were going to have more calves. One of the cows was named Leapy because she was a fence jumper. She had the biggest set of teats (about three inches across at the top); and you had to somehow squeeze them partially, not let go, then you could actually milk her by squeezing the rest of the way and then release partially, then squeeze and so on until she was empty.

You couldn't just start milking those things; it took preparation. Then to top that off, since she was a fence leaper and all the fences had barbed wire, she was always cut badly; and she would tend to kick when it hurt, which seemed to be every time you milked her. With her, it was pull up the stool, start trying to milk her, pick yourself and the stool back up, adjust the hand squeeze, and try again! Sometimes, she managed to spill all the milk.

I did not like to milk cows, her especially, but I would bet I never had a better hand grip than when I did! The grip also helped in carrying the five-gallon buckets of water when we needed to, like for watering the calves in the barn or hauling it to the potato patch. Sometimes, I used my wagon (one of the few toys I had) for that, but a lot would spill on the way either way I did it. But with the wagon, some would spill into it and still arrive with enough to water the plants.

In the summer, we kept the cows up in the mountain pasture during the day and in the south pasture at night. Whenever it rained in the summer and we went to get the cows in the mountain pasture, we would find them in the densest underbrush they could find and would be totally soaked by the time we got home. Some of the cows had bells on them, but when it rained, they didn't move at all so we would have to look in every nook and cranny we could think they would be and always found them in the last place we looked! But of course, it would have proved we were insane if we kept looking for them after finding them! Eventually, that will make sense!

If you saw the movie *Alien*, you were probably horrified to watch a critter emerge from a person's abdomen or chest. Our cows were plagued by something similar but not as dramatic. On a warm spring day, suddenly, the cows would go crazy running around with their tails in the air and just being wild. Heel flies, or tail flies as we sometimes called them, were attacking the cows and were laying eggs on their leg or abdomen. The eggs would hatch, and by some means, the little devils would grow inside the cow and travel to the cow's back and would appear as large lumps on the cow's back that contained ugly-looking grubs about a quarter of an inch thick and about three-quarters of an inch long.

We would put some kind of nasty-smelling powder on the cows back that was supposed to kill them. It smelled like mothballs. We would sometimes squeeze them out when they were ready to come out anyway, and they would leave behind some nasty-looking wounds. It was a relief for the cow but was very gross!

We also had chickens we had to feed every day and gather the eggs. In the summer, the chickens would wonder around the yard, and at night, they would head back to the chicken coop without us having to worry about rounding them up like we did the cattle. We would always feel like we were crawling with little critters after going into the chicken coop to get the eggs, and I am sure it was mostly imagination because of seeing all the daddy longlegs and other spiders and knowing in the back of our minds the chickens were covered with lice. Sometimes, we would catch chickens and cut the heads off for our chicken dinners. They really do run around like chickens with their heads cut off for a while, and they look very weird. I hated doing that and really hated the job of plucking feathers. It is disgusting and itchy work.

At one time, Dad had a bunch of horses, and I remember him chasing them down one time to get them back home after they apparently escaped or something when I was real young. But the two I remember most were two white horses called Jack and Jill. They were mean as heck and would take any opportunity to kick us or crush us on the side of their stall if they could, even while we were being nice to them and giving them feed.

I got kicked a couple of times, once on the thigh and once on the calf, and I can tell you they got your attention fast. They were the team used for pulling hay wagons and for hauling grain to the threshing machine during harvest (covered later) until maybe the early 1950s. Very few of the family attempted to handle them, and Lynn was the one who could do it best. One time, they were acting up and being uncooperative when they were pulling the hay wagon. Lynn told Gordon and I to hang on, and he smacked them several times with the reigns, got them running, and kept them running until they were too tired to run anymore, then they got real cooperative. They kept farting at us as much as they could but were very cooperative. It was a wild ride until then!

Before I was about ten or twelve, horses were used a lot for hauling hay, getting wood to burn in the stoves, and harvesting crops. Most of the heavy work such as plowing, disking, planting, and other work in the fields was done with a John Deere model D tractor. The tractor had two huge cylinders, big flywheel, and since it was a low compression engine, burned special fuel with very low octane. There was a large fuel tank for that in the toolshed, as well as a fifty-gallon gasoline tank for the other engines we used and for starting the John Deere.

We also had fifty-gallon oil drums and five-gallon lidded grease buckets for lubricating the tractor and all the farm equipment. Those five-gallon buckets became buckets for other purposes like carrying water for the cows and calves or the garden and, of course, the infamous slop bucket after they were emptied and cleaned up. The tractor had a little cup with a valve (petcock) on the side of the cylinders that we filled with gasoline and then turn the flywheel to let it get sucked into the cylinders to give a more explosive fuel for starting the engine.

To start the engine, we spun the flywheel by hand using all the strength we could muster. Later, we did get one tractor that had an electric starter on it, but the starter soon crapped out so we were back to starting it by hand again. That was a bit dangerous because the starter was still installed and the flywheel had gear teeth on it. If there was a backfire, we had to remove our hand quickly to keep from getting into the space between the flywheel and starter where the gears were supposed to mesh. We couldn't use gloves to start that one even in winter.

In the pasture on the farm, we had our woodpile; and next to the woodpile a saw was mounted on a wooden frame, anchored to the ground, that I am surprised no one lost any parts on. It had this huge blade that may have been thirty inches in diameter mounted on a fairly large shaft with a pulley that was driven with a belt from the tractor pulley. Neither the pulley nor blade had safety covers, making numerous ways to commit suicide with that contraption!

Two people were required for sawing logs. One would bring the log over (both people would bring it over if it was too heavy for one) and slide it on the saw frame to the blade. One person would hold on the piece being cut off, hoping it wasn't going to be too heavy, then toss it on the pile while avoiding falling on the blade, and get ready for the next piece. Sometimes, the log was too big, would take two cuts, and those would be very heavy. The pile of slippery sawdust made this an even more interesting process!

By the way, we never used ear or eye protection for any farm-work. Our tractor did not have a muffler; therefore, we heard all of the hundreds of very loud engine explosions per minute, the whine of the saw, and the screech of the blade cutting the logs. You could also wound yourself with the tractor with the failed starter, just starting it. *Occupational Safety and Health Administration (OSHA) people would have loved our stuff!*

We had cats on the farm; and among them was a big golden-yellow cat that patrolled the farm for rats, gophers, and mice. He weighed twenty-four pounds and was solid muscle. But he was also very friendly and would purr at the drop of a hat or a scratch behind the ears! He was an expert at catching a stream of milk! Sometimes, when the grass in the yard got deep, you could track his movements by watching the grass wiggle as he was stalking some creature.

We had had a lot of younger cats on the farm too; and sometimes it was fun to watch when they played stalking games, you would see the grass wiggling where they were moving and then suddenly, where the movements converged, a cat would appear leaping up above the grass for a moment. Then off they would go in different directions.

When a cat got wounded, they would not be taken to a vet or anything. It seemed I got the job of "putting them out of their misery," and I did that with the trusty single-shot .22-caliber rifle. I was a pretty good shot with that thing, but I would still do it at close range to make darn sure. It was not fun nor was it sport but just something that had to be done unless you wanted the poor critters to suffer.

We attended a one-room school (eight grades) just the other side of main highway at the northwest corner of the farm. It had a huge furnace in the basement that heated the school through a floor vent. The vent was a great place to get warm after you came back into the school after recess during the winter. Around the furnace was a great place to hide behind when you were playing hide-and-go-seek during recess and probably gave all the kids a good dose of asbestos because it was wrapped with the stuff.

I attended three different schools because my older brothers Marvin and Clair were teaching and I went to their schools one year each besides the one by the farm for six years. Marvin taught there when I was in seventh grade, so I got him twice. Marcia and Margaret attended that school for eight years, so they were both there when he taught there that year. Vernon and Shirley were teachers too but didn't get to have the pleasure of attempting to teach us!

Winter in North Dakota is the most miserable and the most beautiful all at the same time. The sky in North Dakota on cold winter nights with no moon is so amazingly full of stars, it is harder to pick out constellations because all the stars seemed so bright and really close. I had traced the constellation Draco from one end to the other though, and my star maps were pretty well worn by the time I left North Dakota.

I am quite sure the sky there is about the same as when I was a kid since the population outside towns has decreased. Often, the northern lights would brighten the sky and cause some of the dimmer stars to disappear. Meteors were visible quite often. The nights when there was a full moon shining on the snow, and there was a herd of deer coming down from the foothills to get grass under the snow. And little shiny ice crystals falling slowly from the sky was absolutely beautiful.

Often, when we went outside, we could hear the coyotes or wolves howling in the hills. Snow, when it is very cold, squeaks when you walk on it and actually squeals as you drive on it. When it gets very cold, the power and telephone lines get very tight and play a note in the breeze. When there are several wires, they may make different tones because they had not all been the same length, had been stretched differently, and it sounded like they were playing a chord of some kind. When it is about 20 or more degrees below zero, tiny crystals of ice slowly fall out of the air, and it is real pretty as they shine in the sunlight or moonlight.

In the winter of 1947–48, we had about twenty or twenty-five feet of snow in one storm that lasted more than a week. The snowdrifts around the house were so deep that when we climbed up on top, we could look down on the roof of the house. That year, we had tunnels from the house to the barn and to the well from the barn, which was sort of fun for a seven-year-old. The Army and National Guard were called out to help plow the snow with big tracked equipment and, along with the regular snowplows, were busy for a long time.

That was the year when Calvin, who was in eighth grade, and I, a second-grader, had walked to school one morning. The teacher came down the road a short distance—she couldn't go far because the road had big snow drifts—let us get warmed up in the car, and sent us home because she couldn't get the fire to burn in the furnace in the school. She said all it did was to fill the basement with smoke.

When I walked into the house, Mom let out a scream and I found myself back out on the porch where she had taken a can of kerosene that was very cold, poured it over a washcloth, and held it against my cheeks to allow them to thaw gradually, I guess. All I remember at the moment was that it was stinky. All I remember about it later was my cheeks were on fire, and later, I ended up with some nasty sores where they had been frostbitten.

I think Calvin had gotten a bit of frostbite too. Calvin went back outside, checked the temperature, and announced it was 47 degrees below zero. Gee, that matched the number of the year. When we had the usual February heat wave and the temperature reached 20 to 30 degrees above zero, we shed our jackets and basked in the sun again!

Spring in North Dakota was really neat, with the streams of water running down the driveway through the yard and under ice that had formed during the night. The grass would begin to grow right away even through some snow. The first flowers to bloom were crocuses, and the first bird to let us know it was spring was the western meadowlark. Soon, we would be plowing up the approximately a quarter-acre garden for planting. It seemed like a million acres when you had to weed it or water it all by hand with buckets.

At one time, I think it may have been over a half an acre. We grew corn, carrots, potatoes, tomatoes, radishes, turnips, kohlrabi, lettuce, celery, cabbage, peas, beans, onions, rutabagas, beets, cauliflower, watermelon, cantaloupes, strawberries, raspberries, loganberries, and weeds (lots of weeds). The garden, probably about twenty-five or thirty feet by three hundred feet, was between the house and the barn and well; and potatoes, watermelon, and cantaloupes were grown in a field east of the buildings and trees.

We carried five-gallon buckets of water to the plants when there wasn't enough rain, which it seemed there never was. We filled the big cattle-watering tank using the pump on the well. Then, using a little gas engine-operated pump and a hose, we could get to part of the main garden, but it wasn't long enough for much of the garden. Buckets were used for the rest of it. Weeding the gardens was a never-ending job. It was also us younger kids who were tasked with that wonderful job.

In the fall, we would pick peas, beans, carrots, corn, and other vegetables from the garden that Mom would can along with fruit and even some meat in jars and cans (using a machine with a crank that would seal the can lids). She had me sealing a lot of cans, and it was fascinating to see how the can machine worked. It had different-shaped rollers that I would move into position for each sealing step and just keep cranking until the can was sealed.

She used a pressure cooker, steaming away on the cook stove, for canning. We would buy apricots, peaches, plums, bing cherries, and pears in bulk in wooden crates; and she would can them in jars. I liked the bing cherries the best. Another goodie was rhubarb and strawberries canned together. We had lots of blueberries too, which we had picked up in the hills. She made jams, jellies, and marmalade in small jars and filled melted wax on top to seal them.

Carrying wood from the woodpile to the house for the stoves used for cooking was one of the chores for us younger ones. I may as well insert this here because we are talking about chores and sometimes, we wounded ourselves doing chores; but we would have to be close to death before we would see a doctor because we didn't have the money for that. One day, after the school term had ended, Marcia, Margaret, and I were collecting; and I was cutting up dead branches from the trees north of the house.

There was a dead branch still on one tree, which I took a swing at with the axe. It bounced when it hit the branch instead of breaking it off as I expected it would. I lost a bit of control of the axe, and it ended up cutting the flesh on my left ankle right at the ankle bone. I think it may have chipped the bone too. As I limped to the house with my shoe filling with blood, the girls, not realizing I was almost mortally wounded, were yelling at me to take some of the wood in which I was in no mood to respond to.

Mom did her best with Lysol (I think) and some bandages, but the pain kept getting worse; and the wound was getting to look very ugly, swollen, and purple. Finally, at about midnight, we went to Bottineau to the doctor, who was already pissed off because he had been called to his office to take care of someone else and then had to wait for us to get there. I'm not sure if he kind of took it out on me or if he would have had to treat it the same no matter when it happened.

He gave me a tetanus shot, then poured white powdery crystals onto the wound and proceeded to scrub the powder into it with a large Q-tip type of thing. OMG did that hurt! He grumbled about a bad infection preventing him from stitching it up and warned us that if we saw any kind of red or purplish line appearing on my leg, to come back to town immediately, not to him but to the hospital. I think somewhere in his grumbling was mention of losing a leg for less horrible-looking wounds.

To a twelve-year-old kid, that is pretty scary talk. It took about two months before it was totally healed, and during that time, I got out of lots of chores because almost anything I did would open it up and cause it to bleed. There were a few other times I got too sick to do chores, and now I know that I was actually having appendicitis but survived each time. There will be more about that later.

In the summer, it was still daylight at nine in the evening, and the nights were hot until about three in the morning and sometimes didn't cool off at all. I remember a hawk; we called the night hawk because in the evening, as it was getting dark, we heard it put on the brakes with its wings spread as it was diving after something it considered good to eat. The sound made by the wings was similar to a truck engine breaking, only higher frequency. I often wondered whether the hawk had to kill the prey or was it frightened to death before it was grabbed! Fireflies were a rare but interesting sight. I never caught any, but I did try.

The summer thunderstorms were unbelievably fierce also. If it had been a hot day, in the evening you would see the dark clouds appear in the west. They would move in real fast, and the rain would pour down seemingly by the buckets for maybe a half hour or an hour. The thunder would get horrendously loud and arrive almost simultaneously with the lightning, then the rain would move on to the east and the rainbows would appear as the sun came out again.

We could get four to six inches of rain that way in just a short time. After that, our road and part of the yard would be muddy, and it would be really humid as the water evaporated in the heat again. I am not sure why Mom and Dad let us run around in our underwear in the rainstorms when I was little, but it was a lot of fun. They would call us into the house when the lightning got close. Maybe it was one less chore they would not have to do to give us baths.

Our house had lightning rods, which are designed to bleed static electricity into the air so the house doesn't get hit by lightning. They apparently work. One of them was a wind direction indicator with an arrow that turned into the wind and had N, E, S, and W mounted on an *X*-shaped piece of metal below the arrow.

One year in July, I don't remember the year, we woke up at about seven in the morning to the temperature already at 85 degrees and expected a very hot day. By noon, the temperature had dropped to about 70 degrees, and by four, it was raining a very cold rain, which then turned to sleet. By the next morning, the trees had about six inches of ice all over them, and some branches were broken from the weight.

Telephone lines and power lines had grown to about four to six inches in diameter with the ice coating and of course some of them were down. Icicles had formed on the eves, and everything looked really beautiful. Most of the grain crops were in pretty bad shape. For days later, you could hear the noises of the big chunks of ice that fell off trees as it melted. Guess you never know what to expect in North Dakota.

3

Bigger Chores and More Things

In the spring, we plowed the fields and seeded them with wheat, barley, oats, and sometimes flax plus some alfalfa for cattle feed. We had a three-bottom plow, a disk or harrow, and planter, which we used in that order with the old John Deere two-cylinder tractor (the one without a muffler) and then prayed for rain but not too much.

After a day of working with that tractor, your ears would be ringing and you would feel little tingly sensations all over from the vibrations! It was always fun to watch the tractor blow smoke rings when it misfired, which would go way up into the air. It was really neat when it went *bang-bang* and blew a smoke ring through a smoke ring. Sometimes, it would be distracting though, so we kind of had to force ourselves to watch where we were going too.

Whenever we were out in the fields, we were always followed by seagulls, which may seem strange because North Dakota is nowhere near the sea. There are a lot of lakes, water in ponds, and potholes though; and I guess they hang out there when they weren't following us around. Because we did not have irrigation systems, we depended on the rain to make our crops grow, and sometimes there wasn't quite enough of that for good crops.

*****

Haying season would arrive in July or August. We mowed the hayfields using a cutting bar mower pulled by the tractor. The mower blade was driven by the mower wheels, and any time it moved, it moved the cutting blades if it was in gear. So we needed to make sure to disengage it before doing anything at the cutter bar. We then let the hay dry out and raked it into piles which we hauled over to a spot where we stacked it.

We had this rake from hell we pulled with the tractor with some poor guy sitting on a metal seat on the rake, trying to keep the tines on the ground in spite of having a horrendous large pile of hay we were dragging. Guess who got to sit on the rake when I was old enough for this type of recreation! I had to put lots of pressure on a foot pedal which kept the tines down, then when it was time to drop the load, I'd have to trip some tangs into an internal gear on the wheels, get my foot out of the way, and use a lever beside the seat to assist the wheels in lifting the tines because now that we wanted them to, they were reluctant to raise by themselves because of the load!

The wheels would skid a bit. When we hit a high spot on the ground and dragged too much on the tines or the load got too heavy to hold, the foot pedal would kick back, almost launching me off the seat. The lever would hit me on the elbow if it was in the way when this happened. Okay, the fun isn't over yet. One guy climbs up on the stack after we have a pile of hay on each side of it while the other guy pitches the hay up to him to spread it out on the stack.

As it gets higher and higher, it gets tougher to pitch the hay up, and the guy on top has to catch the hay to pull it up. This is truly itchy and scratchy sort of work from the dust and hay getting inside your clothes. We would become very grimy from this form of recreation. To make sure the hay didn't get wet inside the stack, we would round the top of it to make it shed rain and put several pieces of twine over the stack tied to some loose fence posts for weight to keep the top of the stack from blowing in the wind. Stacking hay was the most miserable job other than trying to milk Leapy!

To make matters worse, we would watch in envy as our neighbor Eddy drove his little Ford tractor around his hayfield and stack the hay using a hydraulically operated fork-type contraption made for this kind of work. He used a rake similar to ours to create the little stacks to pick up with his stacker, but his rake was also operated by hydraulics. I think our stacks were prettier than his though!

Just before fall harvest every year, while I was a little but very curious guy, Dad and Olaf Guttu would get together and spend several days putting new bearings (some made out of wood) and other things that needed repair on the old threshing machine and the grain binder. Usually, there were belts and chains that needed fixing or replacing, and all the bearings got greased. I would have loved to mess around in that grease at my age then.

The grain binder had some canvas belts about four feet wide with wooden slats across them that took the grain from the cutting bar into the mechanism that tied it into bundles with twine, and those belts would usually need to be replaced also. It was all fascinating to me. The grain binder was also wheel driven like our mower.

Fall would arrive, the trees would be turning beautiful colors, and the green grain fields would turn yellow or golden colored. Up in the hills, the colors were amazing with all the different types of trees and bushes changing to almost all the colors of the rainbow. Now, it was harvesttime, and Dad and/or my older brothers would go out with the grain binder that cut the grain and tied it into bundles with twine.

It was a two-man job with one driving the tractor and one riding and monitoring the binder and controlling when it dropped a pile of bundles. But someone, and I think this may have been Marvin, had installed a kit that allowed a single person to drive the tractor from the binder seat. It had some very long rods and levers and an extension for the steering wheel. It was quite a contraption and probably very dangerous.

We younger ones would head out there, pick up the bundles, and stack the half a dozen or so in each pile into little teepee-shaped piles called *shocks* with the grain ends on top. Sometimes, the twine came off the bundles, and we would have to collect the loose grain and rebundle it with the twine. Soon, the fields would be covered with these shocks. There the grain would dry out and get ready for threshing. It was *shocking* to realize how much work went into harvesting our crops. Field mice would usually find those shocks a great place to build nests and have babies under them.

Threshing the grain began when it was dry enough, and some neighboring farmers would get together with teams of horses and wagons. Dad would set up the threshing machine facing away from the wind either on the field on our farm or one of the other farmer's fields, depending on whose crops were ready. The tractor would be placed about forty feet from the thing with a huge heavy flat belt (probably twelve inches wide or more) connected to drive pulleys.

Since the pulley on the threshing machine needed to turn counterclockwise, there was a twist in the belt to accomplish that. The belt hung almost to the ground in the middle, and I remember that that was where Dad would step over the belt while it was zipping around, driving the thrashing machine when he wanted to get from one side to the other. I was quite sure, since I was only four or five years old, if I had tried that, I probably would have gone for a fast ride!

The belt moving that fast scared me a little. He would very carefully adjust the speed of the machine using the throttle on the tractor and check the rotation of the main pulley using a stopwatch and a turns counter. By the time he got everything perfect, the crew would have loads of grain waiting to pull up to the machine. The bundles of grain were tossed unto the feeder device (hopefully with the heads of the grain fed first to avoid loss of the grain when the chopper cut the twine holding the bundles together).

It was always fascinating to watch the machine blasting the straw out of the big tube at the front of the machine and making a huge straw pile. We used our straw for bedding for the cattle in the barn in the winter. There were usually a couple of trucks to haul the grain to wherever it was to go, either into town to the grain elevators or to a granary on the farm. Sometimes, Dad used a makeshift bin made out of chicken wire, fence posts, and straw to hold the grain when we ran out of space for it and the prices were too low to haul it into town (I think that was the reason).

Usually, I was out there in the field watching all the action because I wasn't in school yet because we didn't have kindergarten at that time. Because I was just a little guy, I guess Mom thought I shouldn't be out there, but Dad said that he liked it because I always told him when the big main belt was about to come off. Then, he would take a pitchfork, stab it into the ground next to the belt, and use it to push the belt back onto the middle of the pulley on the tractor or the threshing machine as needed.

When our horses pulled up to the machine, Jill had to be closest to it because Jack would have nothing to do with that contraption. I guess Dad had tried it once with Jack next to the thrashing machine; and once was enough because, by the time he got the team stopped, they were halfway across the field. During harvest, Mom and the girls were busy preparing five meals a day: breakfast, morning lunch, dinner, afternoon lunch, and supper as we called them at the time. I got to eat with the threshing crew, and I really think I ate more than they did. It was hungry work watching all the activity.

Maybe this was a psychic thing for me at four or five years old (or not), but I disliked one of the men of the crew the moment I saw him. He kind of freaked me out a little, and I purposely avoided being near him. I couldn't put my finger on what I thought was wrong, but I felt something wasn't right about him. The only thing I liked about him was he had named one of his horses Fartblossom, which I thought was funny.

Then one day, I felt a hand going up the back of my pants leg and a gruff voice saying, "I want to feel your legs." I pulled away fast and ran. I hadn't seen him come up behind me and kneel down. Later, I found out he had hit on my sisters too. I really couldn't understand why a married man would be messing around with a little kid and young girls like that, but there is crap like that happening all the time. I never told anyone about what happened, and if I had, I suspect Mom would not have let me go out there.

When I got older, harvesttime wasn't as much fun because then I had to do some of the work, like shoveling the grain inside one of the granaries. And just before we retired the old machine, I even pitched the bundles off the hay wagon into the machine for a short time when I wasn't in school. That is when we were running out of threshing crew because one by one, the farmers around us got combines which made harvesting a two-man job—one to run the combine and another to drive the truck to haul the grain.

That is when the farmwork on the various farms stopped paying for all the expenses, and Dad increased his other enterprises selling Wards products and calendars, etc. We were probably the last ones in the neighborhood to get one of the new machines, a used one of course, because we still had a few farmers that didn't have the new machines. We used combines for long enough to have had two of them, one of which was a little green compact one and the other a tall silver-colored one.

Even though they had their own engines to power the inner workings, ours were the type you pulled with the tractor. Some of the more well-to-do neighbors got the self-propelled ones. I hauled some grain into town to the grain elevators after I got my driver's license. I think I may have done that a few times before I got my license too.

After harvest, we let the cattle roam the fields because there was always stuff left for them to eat, especially in the hayfields. We still had to round them up for milking, and at night, they stayed in the pasture on the farm. A funny thing would happen in the stubble on the fields after harvest, and it had rained. As you walked in the stubble, it would go into your pant legs and scratch, and sometimes, it would squirt you on the leg with water as you stepped on it.

That is surprising and disgusting at the same time, especially if it is getting cold out. Sometimes, the cows would find a plant we called Frenchweed, and when they ate it, it made them and their milk smell worse than real strong garlic. The milk and cream were unusable if they ate it, and of course, the cows loved the stuff.

Our barn had several stalls where we kept the cattle chained in the winter or for milking every day. There was a center aisle with gutters and stalls on both sides and feed troughs for feeding them on each side just like most barns, but certainly not as modern. We put straw in the stalls every day and cleaned out the crap from the gutters. One stall near the door of the barn was set aside to hold straw for bedding for the cattle and horses. A couple of the stalls had been boarded up to make calf pens.

Speaking of calves, we had to teach them to drink from a bucket. We would take milk to them in the buckets as well as attempt to feed them hay. To get them to drink, we would let them suck on the middle two fingers slightly spread and slowly lower the hand with calf attached into the bucket. Sometimes, as soon as they got down into the bucket and touched the milk, they would whip their heads up and we had to make sure our face wasn't in the way. I learned that the hard way with firsthand experience.

Sooner or later, they would start drinking on their own and we could eventually get them weaned from milk and start them on water. In the winter, the pens had to wait to be cleaned so they got higher and higher, and sometimes, we had to add boards. In the spring, we would clean out the calf pens that by then were really ripe under the top layers. In fact, they would steam from the heat generated by decomposition of the poop and straw. What a wish-a-clothespin-on-the-nose-would-be-comfortable kind of job that was!

Sometimes, we hauled the manure from the stalls or calf pens out to the fields and spread it out, or we would dump it on a manure pile west of the barn. And that was becoming quite a pile. It mostly depended on the weather what we did with it.

The west side of the barn had a stone wall about eight feet high, and there was a hill on that side right up against the wall. We hauled hay or alfalfa in from the haystacks using the same hay wagons that had been used for the harvest and pile it in the storage area at the north end of the barn. It was actually a huge room taller than the rest of the barn where hay was just piled on the ground.

The lower west side of this room against the hill was a continuation of a stone wall that was the west side of the barn. There was a doorway high up on the inside of the west wall that was just above the height of the wagon we used to haul hay when it was on the hill behind the barn, which was highest in that area. We pulled the wagon up there either with horses or John Deere tractor and pitched hay into the big room through that door. The loading and unloading of the wagons were done by hand using three- or four-tined pitchforks.

There was a belt-driven grain grinder on the east side of the hay room with a small door beside it to get access for the belt to the pulley on the tractor outside to drive the thing. There were bins for ground barley and oats beside the grinder. This was also itchy work as was most of the farmwork, as you had to shovel the grain into the thing and shovel the ground grain from the grinder to the back of the bins until they filled up.

In the winter, the cattle would have hay and ground feed which we hauled to their stalls twice a day. Since it was normally very cold, we only let the cattle out to get water a couple times a day in the watering tank next to the well, and if it was extremely cold, we hauled the water in buckets to them from the well. When it was 20 degrees below, the water would freeze too fast in the water tank, and we always had to chop ice out of it. So sometimes, it was easier to haul the water in the buckets. We always had to water the calves with buckets because there was no way we could let them run loose to get water on their own.

Late fall was the time we would butcher some steers and pigs to supply meat for the winter. Usually, the meat was taken into town to a butcher shop, and for part of the meat, the butcher would cut it up and store it for us in a meat locker. Some of the pork was actually stored at home in a pork barrel and covered with smoked salt. That smoked salt was delicious, and when a ham was taken out, that was glistening with a coating of salt you almost wanted to lick some off. But we were not allowed to do the ham-lick maneuver!

Farming was miserable, hard, and constant work with very little time for fun stuff. I had to make every moment we didn't have something we had to do to make whatever toy or contraption I wanted or to play with one I had already made. I am glad I grew up that way because I can appreciate what I have now. Dad took advantage of the soil bank where you got paid not to grow crops, so in 1957, we moved off the farm into the huge city of Carbury (population of fifteen, I think, at that time after we moved there). Of course, Dad had to share what he got with Grandma.

What's really funny is to think of what each person will think of as "the good old days" because my good old days were there on the farm. As miserable as it sometimes was, I wouldn't have had it any other way. We may have been poor financially, but we were rich in having a hardworking but loving family. None of us ever saw the inside of a jail cell, at least that I know of.

It's shocking to see what kids have these days, and most are not satisfied. But then I think about the fact that it was my generation in free countries but mostly the good old USA that developed the technology that made all that stuff possible. And speaking of the good old USA, everything we had when I was a kid was made in it. The only foreign stuff I had seen was John Shelton's Volkswagen. I remember the first imports from Japan were pretty much junk, but after several years, most of the really good stuff was made in Japan, especially electronics. Now almost everything is made in China. I want "Made in USA" back again.

I have to add something to this chapter because now that we are in the midst of the COVID-19 virus mess, I have learned about how much—more than I had previously known—we depend on other countries for most everything. What imbeciles thought it was a good idea to have our pharmaceuticals (unless they were developed in foreign countries) and medical personal protective equipment made in any foreign country?

What the (place I don't really believe in as I explain later) were they thinking? I guess money is the root of all evil, but now I have to add it is the root of all stupidity as well. I thought long ago it was stupid to have our computers and a lot of software made or supplied from outside of the USA. I could go on and on, but I'll just kick my soapbox aside and go on with the book.

4

Some Early Experiences

When I was very young, Vivian and I were sleeping in one bed. I think she had babysitter duty or something, and we had unexpected visitors during the night. I woke up with severe pain on my left ear and blood all over my cheek and the bed. Some rats had gotten into the house, maybe because of the winter being especially severe, and they decided they needed a snack so they took some chunks out of my ear.

Sis had gotten bitten on her nose, but I don't think there was any evidence of it later. She may have been spared some damage because I was making enough noise to scare them off. I have the ragged edges on my ear that proved to me later that it had actually happened and wasn't just a bad dream. This was my earliest memory of anything. This event caused Dad to find out about rat poisons and to buy rat traps. I remember later we used a rat poison called d-CON, but I'm not sure what was available when I was a baby.

I do remember being in a crib and having mumps with cheeks all swollen. Another memory was very painful. I had a little blackboard with foldup legs which I was carrying one day when I fell on top of it. Unfortunately, I had my left hand third finger in the foldup legs, and with my weight and the scissors action, it almost removed the flesh from the tip of my finger. The doctor wanted to amputate the finger, but Mom wouldn't have any part of that. She was determined to save my finger. The scar is very visible, curving around the tip of my ring finger, but thanks to Mom, I still have it. If she hadn't done that, I would only be able to count to nine and a half!

When I was a child and even in my teens, whenever I was lying in bed and had a fever from whatever illness I had, I would hallucinate a big ball-like object slowly coming closer to me, twisting back and forth and pressing down on my body. Then it would move away and repeat the whole thing again. It scared the crap out of me every time. Then it happened once as an adult, but this time, I was determined to figure out why I had it happen.

I had an aha moment when it came to me what it was. It was Dad's bald head. I had seen him do that maneuver with my nieces and nephews. Some of them had laughed, but others had just looked terrified even though they seemed to laugh. I never experienced it again after I figured it out. Seems all early memories (before about five years of age) are of bad things that happened.

One of my first normal memories when I was five years old was waking up with some strange person snoring like a diesel locomotive next to me in my bed. The locomotive hadn't been there when I went to bed and I was puzzled about it, but the smell of cooking bacon drew me downstairs to where Mom was making breakfast. So down I went.

A little while later, the source of the locomotive sounds came down the stairs, and Mom ran over to him and gave him a big hug. It was my brother John, back from England where he had served as an aircraft mechanic in the Army Air Corps. Marvin in the Navy and Vernon in the Marines hadn't gotten home yet. By the way, the reference to diesel locomotives was only to illustrate the sound. We still had steam ones in our area when I was a little kid, and I was fascinated by those things.

I was a normal kid when I was born but somehow didn't get all the nutrients I needed to remain normal, and I developed some bone deformity. Apparently, I slept on my stomach and hugged a little panda bear named Andy Panda under my chest. As a result, my chest became caved in, in the shape of my arm and the blob that was my bear. The doctor said I had rickets. Part of the problem may have been my hatred for milk (according to Mom) and the fact that I was bundled up like an Innuit (well, maybe not that much) even when the weather was hot.

Guess Mom didn't want us to get sunburn. When I was in about third-grade, I remember doctors and nurses coming to the school to give us all physicals and shots for various diseases. The doctor did a lot of complaining to Mom about my condition, which he said had been totally avoidable. He knew I was normal when I was born. Of course, I never even thought about my condition until puberty when I started getting interested in the female half of our species, but I will go into that later.

*****

Running around in a thunderstorm in our underwear was a lot of fun! I know I wrote it before, but this is a lame way of introducing the next topic. Not sure why Mom let us do it, but us three youngest ones would have a ball trying to splash as much as possible in almost a flash flood during afternoon thunderstorms. I think she may have thought the lightning rods on the house would bleed off the close stuff and make it safer for us to have our fun. Or did she? Maybe she thought there are too many kids around! Just kidding. I think she knew nothing bad was going to happen because she was psychic. See, there is the topic!

Yes, I said she was psychic. One time, she got all upset and told Clair to go rescue Vernon and told him where he would find him in his car which had stalled out. It was winter, and being overdressed for a date was something Vernon would not have done. He would have quickly frozen to death since it was really cold that night.

The evening had started out fairly mild weather wise, but it had suddenly turned very cold. And very cold in North Dakota is very often below zero. Clair found him exactly where she told him he would be and brought him home. Now you're probably thinking Vernon had called home, but remember that cell phones didn't exist in those days nor were there call boxes. Most farm homes had one phone and were quite far apart, so he probably would not have made it to anyone's farmhouse. Now, people keep blankets or extra clothes in their cars in the winter because you never know when they will be needed.

Mom told me about some out-of-body experiences she had when she was really sick as a young girl. In one instance, she said she met with dead relatives who told her it wasn't her time to leave the earth; and in another, she saw a person she thought was Jesus who simply looked at her for a moment, shook his head, and turned and walked away. She tried to follow but just ended up awake and feeling better. She had told some of us that she would have some surgeries and be okay, but *"when they operated on her head she would die."*

Having a psychic mother means you don't have much opportunity to get away with much and you learn to be honest most of the time. She rarely scolded and never spanked, but the disappointment she showed when we did do something wrong was enough. I feel she made me a better person just by being the person she was. She did say insanity reigns where I was, which I'm wondering if I took maybe too seriously later on when strange things seemed to happen to me and around me. My own psychic experiences throughout my life did make me wonder if insanity truly rained where I was at times.

Mom was noted for her piano and organ playing. For years, she was the organist in our Lutheran Church and could make great music even better on either the organ or the piano. I made up some music one time, which she played for me. It sounded awful, so maybe I was not a composer by a long shot. Her music was cut short one day when Dad and someone else (it may have been the piano tuner) were moving the piano.

She was putting a spacer under one corner to make the piano level, but the wheel slipped off onto her thumb. The crunch was quite loud, and it was the first time I heard Mom cry. It was a sad day for all of us. Eventually, she did play the piano again, but it was hard for her because of arthritis and the remaining stiffness in her thumb. It probably never healed right.

We all lived on the farm even though Dad never wanted to be a farmer. He had wanted to be a Lutheran minister; but Grandma would have none of that, needing someone to continue farming to ensure that she would have an income after the death of her first husband, my grandpa John. She married again, and I really don't think she needed the income from the farm, at least while he was alive.

I don't remember her second husband as she must have caused his early demise just by being who she was before I could be aware of his existence. I don't remember her ever smiling. When we went to visit her, she would be around long enough to say a few words to Mom. Depending on the time of day, she would have some coffee with Mom and Dad, give us kids come cookies and milk, then her and Dad would adjourn to another room to discuss farm business.

One of the business discussions, I think, was the fact that the Rural Electrification Administration (REA) was putting up power lines near the farm, and I think Dad wanted to put in wiring in the buildings to take advantage of it. But—there was always a but—we would have to put in several power poles along one road and across the farm property to the buildings, all of which would cost more money.

I really don't know how I know, but I know Grandma was the one who objected to the cost. As a result, we continued to live in primitive conditions with no running water, kerosene lamps, gasoline lanterns for light, and a pristine view of the absolutely beautiful night sky with no light pollution. See, there is usually an upside to even the most disgusting conditions.

Our neighbor Eddy had electricity, but more importantly, he had a new thing called TV. When I was twelve to sixteen years old, I would sometimes walk to his house and watch some shows with him that he liked to watch. *The Eddy Arnold Show* was his favorite, I think, and it became one of my favorites too. I still don't know if he liked the company or not, but he never refused it.

Sometimes, on moonless nights, when the sky was overcast, when I went home after seeing several shows, it would be so dark that I couldn't see a thing. Not thinking ahead of time to bring a flashlight, nor was I psychic enough—yes, it turns out I was a bit psychic too—to just take one, I would have to feel my way along the road and try to stay in one of the ruts we always had on the gravel roads.

Finally, I would have some dim light from our house windows, and it made it easier to navigate the rest of the way. The trip home was at times made more exciting because I would hear the wolves and coyotes in the hills. I guess they didn't need moonlight to get excited about something. Sometimes, they sounded very close. The trip home was a bit over three-quarters of a mile. I'm probably very lucky we didn't have mountain lions when I was a kid, but I understand they are back in that area now.

5

My First Psychic Experiences

Because of events beyond Dad's control, as I mentioned before, the farm wasn't making enough to cover all the expenses; so he had a couple of other businesses going as a salesman. He sold Wards (not associated with Montgomery Wards) products to anyone who would buy them. Of course, we used a lot of the products too; and he had sample calendars, stationary, business cards, and posters from several companies for businesses to order to display or give out to customers.

He had several businesses he would make the rounds to see if they needed to order any more of them, and when I was about eleven years old, Dad and I went into town to make the rounds. I found the calendars offered to bars and liquor stores interesting later on because they were of the shapely pinup types, but I wasn't interested in that at the time. We had spent a good part of the day together doing this, of course stopping for ice cream at some point. Maple nut was my favorite flavor, and I could still taste it when we went to a jewelry shop and got orders for some business cards and calendars.

While we were there, for some reason, a certain wristwatch became of interest to Dad. The jeweler said that someone had dropped it off for repair and never came to pick it up. He would sell it for the cost of repair, ten dollars, which Dad thought was really a good deal; so he bought it for me. It had a fairly small wrist strap with several holes, and it fit me perfectly. I admired my new possession, which had an interesting brand name, Cauni, as I think it was spelled.

I discovered right away that if you weren't careful, you could overwind it and it would stop running until you rocked it back and forth to make the movement keep moving. It would start running normally after a short while doing this, and the spring got unstuck. I was careful how much I wound it after this happened a couple times. I would always check it periodically to see if the hands had moved, not often to actually see what time it was, although I did check that sometimes too.

One morning, Vernon got interested in the watch for some reason, and he watched me check it a few times, then asked what time it was. He seemed amused that I actually looked at the watch to tell him the time because he had just seen me check it seconds before. He then asked if he could borrow the watch because he had to go out plowing a field and wanted to know when to stop for lunch and see how much progress he was making.

Being a good guy seemed to be the best course of action, so I took off the watch and handed it to him. The thought *I'LL NEVER SEE THE WATCH AGAIN* entered my brain all of a sudden (*capital*, italic letters even), then was replaced by *I'll see it again, but it won't be mine*. I was amazed at the certainty I felt about it, and I wanted to grab it back but didn't. I knew I had lost the watch forever, but for some reason, I felt it was what was supposed to happen.

That evening, after we were done with supper, as we called the evening meal, I asked about the watch. He told me he was very sorry, but when he had reached back to trip the plow, he had caught the watch on a part of the tractor. It had pulled the retainer from the band, and the watch got plowed under. Of course, I didn't believe him because I knew that, sooner or later, I was going to see the watch again.

Maybe a couple months passed when we had occasion to visit with Marvin's future in-laws. His father-in-law was in a wheelchair and was partially crippled. I think he had polio when he was young. He had dropped a small blanket on the floor when it got caught under a wheel, and I went over to help retrieve it when the thought entered into my brain, *Look at his watch*. I looked and saw the brand name, Cauni.

I then knew exactly what had happened. Marvin had promised to have the watch fixed, had dropped it off at the jewelers, and forgot about it. He probably remembered when he saw I had the watch then cooked up the scheme to get it back with Vernon's help. I accepted the fact that it was not my watch as I knew whose it was and had been all along and had no hard feelings. I did, however, never forget it happened because it was a very startling first hint that Mom was not the only psychic in the family, and it turns out all of us had a little bit of it. Later on, I bought my very own Mickey Mouse watch which, if I still had, would be worth a fortune now.

My second startling experience in the psychic world was quite weird and actually scared me somewhat. I was about eleven years old. Chores were done for that morning, and I had been on my usual quest to find something or make something to play with. So I had been at the big stone pile; and while I was there, I saw Dad, Mom, Vivian, Shirley, Marcia, and Margaret get in the car and leave to go to town for shopping.

I was alone on the farm now but still had lots of pebbles collected for target practice with my slingshot made with a *Y*-shaped stick and some old inner tube rubber, so I spent about another half hour out there then went to the house. I found some of Calvin's science fiction books and was upstairs reading one for maybe two hours when I heard the car come down the driveway and park in front of the house. I heard the engine stop, car doors open and close, my sisters talking, the door open, and the noises downstairs of people moving around. Then, it got very quiet.

Wondering whether they brought home some more of those delicious black cherries, I meandered downstairs to find no one there, nor did I see any bags of groceries. I went outside thinking maybe they were bringing stuff in. There was no car and no family in sight. By now, the hair was standing up on the back of my neck. *What the heck just happened?* I gathered as much wits about me as I could with all this insane rain falling on me, figuratively speaking, and went back to reading.

I found I had a hard time reading and read the same paragraph several times still not remembering any of what I was reading. About fifteen minutes passed, and I heard all of the above scenario play out again exactly as I heard it the first time. It didn't miss a beat. It was all there. I waited, starting to shake all over wondering if it was "still raining insanity." But this time, the sounds continued, so I meandered downstairs again and found everyone home. And yes, they had gotten two crates of those delicious black cherries.

We would eat some of them, and Mom would can the rest. After this sort of thing happened several times, I started expecting it, so I would wait to make sure things actually happened and the sounds didn't stop before I would do anything. Sometimes, when I was sitting my two younger sisters and it happened, I asked if they heard anything; and they said no most of the time. They started to experience it too as they got older. Funny thing, I can't remember what book I was reading, but the rest of it seemed to have happened not long ago even though it's been almost seventy years.

Many times, when I was going to the mountain pasture to get the cows or when I just went up there to pick berries or get away from it all, I found I would take the south side trail around the grove of trees, which was actually out of the way, but would see the reason I had unconsciously done it as I reached the gate and looked back down the north side trail, the direct route. I had, without preknowledge of the reason, actually avoided some encounters with wild creatures crossing that trail, some of which could have been quite nasty.

The critters included a porcupine, several times skunks (the young ones are especially bad), one time a female badger with two cubs—wow, when I think about that one, I get the shivers—a raccoon, and a cute little fox. I think being out in the daytime for badgers is very unusual, but it happened. She may have been moving her cubs to safety or something. I've heard that human encounters with female badgers with cubs don't usually go well for the human or the badger if the human is armed, which I wasn't. Any one of those critters can be quite mean under the wrong circumstances.

I seemed to have a knack for finding useful things even if it meant absentmindedly going out of my way and/or into awkward places. I had seen a dragline or digging machine that used a scoop attached to two cables, a drag cable, and lift cable. It had the steel structure (boom) to raise the scoop bucket; and it was operated by dropping the bucket hanging from the lift cable, digging end down, then dragging it with the drag cable to scoop up dirt or sand.

When you pick up a load with that thing, the cables had to be kept taut to keep from dropping the load too early, and then slackening the drag cable released the load. Or at least from what I saw, that is how I thought it worked. I decided to build a toy dragline like that one, and I started looking for metal parts to make the thing.

There happened to be some cans and bottles someone—I think it was people who had hunted on the property—had dumped in the southeast corner of our mountain pasture. I looked momentarily at the pile and walked around it into the brush thinking, *What am I doing?* Then I spotted it—a rectangular sardine can which was shaped almost exactly like what I wanted and would take very little work to make it just right.

I know I hadn't seen that can before, and I was surprised as to why I had walked right to it. I built the dragline using the can, solder, wire, thread spools, some cord, a few screws, wood and nails, and was totally satisfied with what I thought was a job well done. The framework I created as a boom, about ten inches long, made of stiff wire, was strong enough that I could stand on it without bending or crushing it. But then, I was fairly light and an adult probably would have crushed it flat. My creation actually worked well in soft dirt or sand. I sometimes wish I still had that thing now because that was the most complicated toy I had ever made.

When I was twelve, Calvin had turned eighteen and decided to join the Army, the seventh and last of us eight boys to go into the service. We got a call from the train depot that there was a bag of his civilian clothes there for us to bring home. I decided that I could walk into town and get it because it was only a seven-mile round trip. I didn't have much to do that day, and I may as well go for a walk.

As I walked along SR-14 toward the mighty village of Carbury, I made sure to walk on the left side of the road facing traffic (of course there wasn't any—traffic that is) and made it in about an hour and a half from home to the depot as I was in no hurry.

The depot agent gave me the bag, and I got a drink of water from the water cooler that was there for passengers if the train ever had any, and I headed back toward home. About twenty minutes or so into the trip home, I found I had absentmindedly crossed the road to the right side, set the bag down, and wandered into the ditch which had a lot of tall grass growing in it.

I thought, *What the heck am I doing?* I had gotten all the way into the ditch by then, didn't see anything that should have attracted my attention, but slipped on something hard. I reached down and pushed aside the grass and found a pint bottle of Seven Crown whiskey. It still had the tax stamp over the lid, so I could tell it had never been opened. I tried to put it into my pocket but decided that it didn't fit well and would be very awkward to carry that way, so I opened Calvin's bag and put it in there when I got out of the ditch.

I made the trip home the rest of the way without detours, facing the nonexistent traffic on SR-14. When I got home, I showed Mom what I had found, thinking she would tell me to give it to Dad. She shocked me when she said, "Share it with your brother." Clair and I shared it a little at a time for maybe a week, and I think it created an even closer bond between us.

6

UFO, Little Old Ladies, Etc.

One really nice evening in 1951 or 1952 ('52, I think) Calvin and I were outside. It was late evening. The clouds to the west still had a little color, and the clouds were only on that horizon so the rest of the sky was clear. Calvin did not remember this when I asked him several years ago, but we saw a fairly bright orange object that passed slightly east of overhead from north-northeast to south-southwest slowly crossing the entire sky.

It took about ten to fifteen minutes to travel from horizon to horizon. It was close enough or large enough that you could see it was sort of egg shaped and appeared about one-fifth the size of the moon in the sky. It seemed to slowly change shape slightly, and it varied slightly in brightness also. I have been trying to verify that someone besides me saw the thing. I thought the verification came quite unexpectedly from Marcia one day on August 18, 2008, when I just happened to ask her if she saw a strange object when she was a kid.

She said she remembered this object, which she saw from the parlor window, and she remembered it because it had scared her. I asked her what color it was, and she said yellowish-red (well to me, that is orange). She would have been five or six years old at the time it was visible. Unfortunately, when I asked her about it again recently in 2018, she describes something quite different now. She may have confused the memory with a fighter jet we had seen flying very close later when we were in school because she said it made noise. That

UFO sure didn't make noise, so I don't have a firm verification that anyone else saw it.

I now think I know what the object could have been. There is an asteroid called Apophis that is going to come close by earth in April 2029. If the asteroid goes through a certain fairly narrow area in space as it passes earth, on the next pass on April 13, 2036, it is predicted it could hit the earth. If not, it will be a close pass again. It now has an orbit that brings it around approximately every seven years, and if you figure eleven orbits, you get seventy-seven years. Eleven orbital passes before 2029 is 1952. Assuming it has an orbit that varied some because of the planets tugging on it, we could have seen it in 1951 or it could have been in the spring of 1952 while Calvin was still at home.

I was excited about it, and that is when I started getting really interested in looking at the sky a lot, then getting my first rotating star map from Edmund Scientific Co soon after it happened. Scientists are supposedly working on plans to give the asteroid a push or a pull to keep it from smacking earth right now and should hopefully have a plan well in advance if it is necessary. It is possible we saw a completely different asteroid too, but it is still a UFO because I don't know what it was or its name for sure!

There was a little old lady that lived in Carbury who was a little scary looking (could never have been a Playboy model for sure) named Ingalive, and I had heard some kids say she was a witch and they seemed to be afraid of her. It turns out she was one of the nicest people you could ever have met, and she had a heart of gold.

She was a real people person who was always concerned about other people. We would see her at the church events or whatever. She did talk with a brogue that made her somewhat hard to understand sometimes. She often visited her neighbors Ole and Jenny in the evenings, and if it got dark out, he would walk her home. One year, as winter was approaching, Calvin and I went to Carbury with Dad's pickup to bring her a couple loads of coal. I think it was 1951 and I was eleven at the time.

The train had brought in a carload of the small-sized coal, which was the kind she could use in her furnace; so we went to the depot, weighed the pickup, and loaded the coal from the boxcar, reweighed, paid for the coal (with her money of course), took it to her house, and shoveled through a small door into her coal bin in the basement. We did this twice, and then she invited us in for some cookies.

We had a long conversation with her about all kinds of stuff, but one thing was a bit humorous. She asked, "How's your-r-r mode-ehr-r-r?" You have to roll the *r* a whole bunch on that one to make it sound right the way she said it!

Calvin answered without hesitation. "Oh. It runs all right."

Now I had a few moments while Calvin was speaking to think about why she would ask about our vehicle, and it dawned on me what she meant. So I said, "She has been feeling a little better, but she still has a lot of headaches." Then, we talked about Mom's health problems, the weather, about our future plans, and what others in the family were doing. It was neat to talk to an old person who seemed genuinely interested in our family and not just making small talk.

Things I learned

Any one of these could have caused Mom to say "Insanity reigns where you are!"

Taking a large board, holding it above your head like a wing, and running off the barn roof is never a good idea!

Do not ever use one rope with a calf tied to each end to round up ones that have gotten out of the pasture. I did, and it is not pleasant. I finally got the two of them cornered and had the rope on one. A moment of insanity took over, and I thought that when I get the one critter back to the pasture, I would be lucky to find the other one again and then I would have to chase it down again. I had just tied the other end of the rope on the second calf and was about to tie the rope close together next to their heads so they could be led together, or so I thought.

I was not fast enough; and they took off in different directions, then the same direction pulling me along, then opposite directions again, hit the end of the rope, then decided to go in opposite directions around me. They both went about 180 degrees. So there I was with a rope around my waist and a calf on each end pulling in opposite directions. I had the presence of mind to try to get out of this mess by pushing the rope down, not up toward my head, so I ended up pulled off my feet when they decided again to work together.

Well, at least it wasn't by the neck! I did finally get the rope tied where I wanted it and got them both to the water tank where they got to drink, then I proceeded to haul the buggers to the pasture. After returning the calves, I untied the knots on the rope and vowed never to prove what Mom had said about me again. I really don't know if I have succeeded in that.

Before you try to see how fast you have to swing a jar of molasses to make the contents fill only the top of the jar, check to see if the lid is on tight first.

Do not, under any circumstances, stick the tip of your tongue against a flagpole to see if the rumors are true that it will freeze to the pole in cold weather. It does, and pulling it off will leave a small piece of your tongue on the flagpole. That was really dumb!

Do not, under any circumstances, break a dud firecracker in half and light it while you are still holding it. It makes a neat flare but will probably flare out both ends, and it causes third-degree burns in about a millisecond.

If you have the urge to see how high you can throw a heavy object straight up, don't. If you do, make sure you can run fast in some direction, which of course I did.

If you decide to run and jump over a barbed wire fence, make sure all parts of your clothes make it over too.

Fishing trip

On October 3, 1957, Clair, our friends Myron Shelton and his uncle John Shelton, and I went on a fishing trip at Lake Metigoshe, North Dakota; and believe it or not, we caught some perch.

We took the fish to the mountain pasture and found a spot in a gravel-bottomed ditch where we could build a fire and cook fish over an open fire. This is the spot I saw the dragline I built a model of for a toy. It had started digging in our pasture in the hills before our neighbor informed them. They were on the wrong property and were supposed to be digging a gravel pit on his land. We must have thought we would catch fish too because we had everything ready as well as enough beer to wash it down and then some for the next day. After we ate that night, we slept under the stars, which was really neat because it was a beautiful night.

The next morning, as we were all waking up, the first words we heard from John Shelton was, "Anybody got a Rolaid?" I don't think anybody did. Anyway, we decided to cook some more fish for breakfast and that was great too, but the rest of the beer was a little warm by then. We had used most of the ice to keep the fish cold. We turned on the car radio and heard the news that Russia had launched Sputnik, the first satellite. All the thing did was to orbit the earth, sending out a beeping radio signal, but it was exciting and a bit disgusting as well because we weren't the first.

President Eisenhower didn't seem concerned about it that much at all. He knew we were working on our own satellite and would launch it when we were really ready to prove we could do some science at the same time. Our rockets seemed to have a tendency to explode. The first one we launched successfully, after a lot of failures, was Explorer I on January 31, 1958; and it had instruments to measure charged particles and to detect tiny meteorite hits. At least we got more science done than the Russians with our first successful attempt.

Beetles—no, not the band

John Shelton knew about beetles before most people did. He bought one of the first Volkswagens we had ever seen. I think everyone kind of laughed at this thing, but I think he knew we were all jealous. After all, where else can you buy a thing that looks like a toy that actually works like the real thing? That car is probably worth a fortune if it is still around somewhere.

Mailman

The mailman was never stopped by weather. Remember that through wind, rain, fire and brimstone, and dark of night, or however that goes, the mail must go through! Anyway, winter in North Dakota was no laughing matter. Sometimes, there were snow drifts as high as houses. Our mailman had a little Model A Ford that he had had modified with these huge balloon tires like some of the off-road vehicles you see today, but on that car, they seemed extra huge. He just drove right over the snowbanks and hardly left a mark on them. We always got our mail.

Skunks

The granary/machinery shed where the tractor and fuel tanks were had an upstairs room above the grain bins with some tools such as axe and knife sharpener, hand-operated corn planter, scythes, rope maker, and such. Clair, I think, and someone, possibly Lynn, decided that skunk pelts would be worth lots of money. No one I had talked to will admit to having anything to do with it, so I have to assume it was them. I am not sure how many pelts they got, but the upstairs room in which the work was done was almost unapproachable for a week and would force a person to leave very soon for several months. The stench was not completely gone for at least two years, or maybe we just got used to it.

Manure pile

I overheard Lynn and Howard discussing making money in various ways. The subject apparently was about the huge pile of manure we had west of the barn, which they thought could probably be sold as fertilizer. At one point, Lynn said, "We could really clean up on a deal like this." The discussion went on for a while, and then Lynn said, "We could make a pile!" That caused enough laughter to end the conversation.

No bull

I did not see this firsthand but was listening closely when the story was related to another member of the family. Reportedly, Calvin had been herding the bull either to or from the pasture (probably because it had gotten out) when it turned on him, put its head down, and started pawing—no, that can't be—*hoofing* the ground. Calvin started backing away, and the bull started snorting and began making its move.

Lynn was in front of the house and saw the action. He reportedly sprinted the 150 yards or so, leaping the fence meant to keep our cattle out of the garden, grabbing a wooden fence post on the way, literally ripping it out of the ground, launching the staples when the fence stretched to the limit, and twanged like guitar strings. He proceeded to use the fence post to convince the bull to leave Calvin alone!

As I said, I did not see this myself, but I did see the hole in the ground left by the post.

Now I don't know how many records were broken that day: hundred-yard dash, possibly the four-minute mile, the high jump, shortest bull fight on record...on and on.

Calvin, at some time, corroborated the story; and I had talked to Vivian about this. And she said, "Yes, it happened just like that."

Clair's automotive

Clair was always doing something with motor-driven contraptions it seems. There was this old truck that he got from somewhere, and it had this super low gear as well as a two-speed rear axle. It had no box, but the cab and frame were intact. But you couldn't turn the engine over at all because it was frozen from sitting around for years.

I think in the back of Clair's mind may have been the idea of getting this thing running, putting big tires on it, and using it as a second tractor. In fact, this is what he said one time. I had my doubts that the thing would ever run. So he took out the spark plugs, poured oil in the spark plug holes, got the tractor hooked up to the thing, and pulled it around the yard until the engine started turning over.

He just kept working on the thing until he had the engine turning freely. He and I worked on it for a couple days getting the plugs cleaned, spark system checked out, flushed out the cooling system, and got it all ready for a test run. It wasn't long before the thing was actually running. He had to do a test to see just how much play there was in the gears.

So we backed it up, put it in the lowest gear, set the rear axle speed to the lowest speed, let the engine idle, and let out the clutch. I think it took about twenty seconds before we saw any movement in the wheels. Well, I think this may have been the only thing Clair had been interested in because that is all we did with it! I have no idea what happened to that old truck!

He owned several Ford Model A cars of various configurations. They were all fun, and I think they were all from around 1928. One of them was a convertible that had the top held on with two bolts and two nails. Pull out the bolts and the nails, lift off the top, and you're ready to go driving with the breeze in your hair. He didn't seem to have that one very long. He would buy and sell the things. I wish I had that one now.

Another Ford Model A he had had only two speeds forward. This is how that came about. When Clair drove, he would use the engine for braking by double-clutching and shifting into lower gears to slow down. Trucks use this method all the time, and it works well.

One Saturday night, he, Calvin, and I were headed into town; and we were approaching an intersection quite rapidly. All North Dakota roads have ditches that are quite deep on both sides. The corner we were approaching on the gravel road also had had a grader working on it, so there was a windrow of gravel maybe six inches deep along the opposite side of the road we were approaching. We were going at a pretty good clip as we approached the intersection, and Clair did the usual shift down. But all we heard was a big bang and gears grinding, and the car didn't slow down. He decided to attempt the turn but thought better of it halfway through because we were going to turn over if he continued, so we went off the side of the road that went at right angles to the one we were leaving.

Now I mentioned that the ditches in North Dakota are deep, but we also had the windrow of gravel to contend with. It caused us to bounce upward as we went over the side, so we were airborne for what seemed a long time but was probably less than two seconds. There is an airplane that astronauts train in that is lovingly called the Vomit Comet. Well, his car gave us the momentary feeling that the Vomit Comet gives the astronauts, except that I hit my head on the top of the car because, being in the back seat, I was also launched upward by the added upward motion over the gravel.

I was not hurt and *not stirred but shaken* a bit. Clair wasn't fazed at all because he didn't even stop the car as we made a U-turn in the ditch. He asked if we were okay, gunned the engine (in low gear by now), and we climbed back onto the road and headed into town. He drove the car with two gears for a long time after that.

He had another Model A that he had stripped the body off it, and it was just the frame with the front part of the car still intact around the engine with the steering wheel and dash still in place (sort of the ultimate convertible). He had taken blocks of wood as wide as the frame and mounted that to the frame and put the seat on them. Somehow, he put floorboards back on the frame so we wouldn't fall out the bottom of the car. He would drive this thing around on the farm, and we even used it to pull some logs out of the hills for firewood one time. It was great fun because it would give a tremendous feeling of speed even if you weren't going fast. When it had rained, it threw mud all over, but that was kind of fun too.

At one time, Clair also had a Pontiac straight-8 that had the biggest hood of any car I ever saw. It had an I-block eight-cylinder engine that was the longest engine I ever saw in a car too. He didn't seem to have it for a long time either. I just think he thought it was fun to have strange-looking cars.

Then, he bought a 1957 Ford Fairlane that was built of a bit lighter material than most of the cars had been up to that time. It was also a longer car. It had a new kind of frame, and I was fascinated by how flexible the car was. We were going about seventy miles per hour on a gravel road that had become very rough because it hadn't been maintained for some time (what we called rubbing board), and I swear the car frame actually flexed several inches. They probably weren't really built for North Dakota gravel highways of the time.

But the ride was a lot smoother relatively than our old Chevy, which was built like a rock and bounced a lot. I am not sure which flexed more, the springs or the body!

He also had gotten a Fordson tractor from somewhere, which was a little bit like a Ford tractor but was an older model. It had steel wheels, and the back ones had these huge cleats. It would have made short work of a paved highway, but not to worry because we didn't have any near our farm at that time.

He, our other brothers, and I also spent some time gathering old metal and hauling it to the scrap metal collection they had for several years in Bottineau. I don't remember if some of the automotive stuff he collected was part of that or not, but it did reduce the fun I had at the stone pile because some of the old car bodies were hauled away. The truck (with scrap metal which was later unloaded) was weighed to see how much we had, and we got so much per pound for it. We unloaded directly into a railroad open top car.

I don't know if you can call this automotive or not, but Clair had me working for him and promised to buy me a bicycle after I had done stuff for him for a while. If I objected to a request or hesitated to do whatever he wanted, he would say, "Red or blue?" So usually, I would do whatever he wanted, and he came through with the bike. It was a great bike; and I only crashed into the trees twice before I got the brake, balancing, and steering all at once figured out. Didn't harm anything but my pride; did get a few scratches and maybe damaged a few of the lower branches of the trees closest to the road!

He also provided the Rambler American that I drove for my first two years of college and bought the Mercury I drove for my last two years at the university and that I drove to my job. I paid him back for the car after "I got rich." Oh, wait a minute, when was that? I really don't remember "rich," but I did finally pay him back.

Helping big brother

When I was a kid and didn't drive the tractor yet, I remember one time the spring had come fairly late and we needed to get the fields plowed to get them planted, so some older brothers had been busy doing just that. Clair decided that the plowing was going to get done even if it meant plowing all night. He had been working in the field for a while after dark and needed to refuel the tractor, so he came into the house and asked if I wanted to ride along "to keep him awake."

Being either dumb or curious, I said yes, and away we went. It was a cold night, so we were wearing jackets. But it still felt very cold, mostly when we were going with the wind at our backs. When we went into the wind, the heat from the tractor engine actually warmed us up, and every once in a while, we would get a blast of exhaust blown back too. With the noise of the tractor, there was really no way to talk, so I don't know how I could do anything to keep him awake.

Actually, I think he kept himself awake by periodically yelling at me, asking if I was still awake! Not only was I awake, but I was hanging on for dear life because my seat was curved (the fender of the tractor), and every now and then, I would stand on the platform between the fenders to get more comfortable and realized that when I got back on the fender, my butt got wet. The dew precipitating on the fender was making it very wet.

It was one of those nights that the northern lights were really active and colorful. The way they moved was fascinating to watch, and I did watch every chance I got to let go and hold up one hand to shield my eyes from the tractor lights. The tractor had bright lights facing front and rear plus the little ones that light up the instrument panel. A few times, I steered the tractor while Clair was looking at them. I think we were out there until about two thirty in the morning, but that field got plowed just like Clair said it would. It was a lot of fun though to "help out" big brother!

Excuse me while I go back in time for some more fun stuff.

Other fun things to do

When I was nine years old, I stayed with brother-in-law Harold and Gretchen on a farm they were renting up by Rolla, North Dakota, during the summer. His dad had a farm in that area too. The barn on his dad's farm had a hayloft that had these fantastic slings for hauling the hay up into the hayloft from the ground.

Harold found a new toy in these things for his brothers Larry and Perry and me. He would lock the mechanism so the rope could be made to hang down in the middle of the hayloft floor but could be pulled up on the pulleys on one end. There was a kind of ladder arrangement at that end for getting up to maintain the slings. One of us would hold on to the rope in the middle that hung down near the floor. Harold would climb the ladder; grab the rope; yell, "Ready? Hang on"; then jump off with the rope in hand. We would go flying up almost to the roof of the barn (twenty-five to thirty feet above the hayloft floor), and then he would lower us slowly to the floor. Better than Disneyland!

On a farm he rented, he or the owner had built a huge squirrel cage that was hooked up to the water pump. His dog Duke, a German Shepherd, would hop into this thing and run like crazy and pump water. The dog loved to do it and got lots of exercise. The squirrel cage seems like something Harold would have done.

On the farm were a lot of gophers, and Harold really wanted to get rid of them. So he told me he would give me a nickel for each one I caught. When I caught them (and they were dead of course), he showed me how to grab them by the tail and fling them away so the tail would come off. To prove I had caught them, I would bring him the tails. So off I went with the traps and got them set in the gopher holes. I would usually catch a couple of gophers in each trap each day, and so I was getting lots of money. Soon, however, we ran out of gophers. I have no idea how many there were, but it was lots of them, and I think Harold may have even regretted making the offer before it was done.

I was a little guy at the time, but I drove his truck (only in low gear). For some reason, he needed his truck to be somewhere that I would meet him. I think he may have been checking fences or something. To drive the truck, I had to get down on the floor, hold in the clutch, shift into gear, release the brake, pull the throttle (it was on the dashboard), let out the clutch, and quickly get up on the seat to steer. Then, I could use the throttle to speed up or slow down. To stop, I had to hop down, push in the clutch and throttle, step on the brake, and pull the hand brake. I didn't hit anything or do any damage, but I got the truck where he wanted it.

One day, when we were going into town for something in Harold's truck, I was sitting next to the door with Gretchen sitting in the middle. We were traveling fairly slow because the road was in such rough shape with potholes everywhere. I was hanging unto a sort of armrest on the door to keep from bouncing around too much. We hit a deep pothole, and somehow, the door swung open with me still hanging on. I was launched out of the truck and rolled into the ditch. I didn't feel any impact at all, just rolling off the side of the road into the middle of the ditch because I was still in sort of a sitting or maybe moved to a fetal position, creating a human ball. I'm not sure which, but I didn't get hurt at all. Harold and Gretchen were all concerned about if I was okay, and I said I was. Actually, I thought it was kind of fun!

The farm had direct current (DC) electricity from a huge bank of batteries. The batteries were charged by a wind charger, so if there was no wind for several days, there was no electricity. The batteries were huge things made by Exide, and they had little balls of different colors that floated or sank in the electrolyte depending on how much charge was in the batteries. When they were charging, they had lots of bubbles rising to the top. I think that was where I first got interested in electricity and things electrical like motors and radios.

The farm had a little stream running through it. In the stream were little crayfish that resembled tiny lobsters. They were only about an inch long. I had never seen them anywhere else in North Dakota, but I verified that there are some of those critters in the state. I wonder what they do in winter when everything is frozen solid because they don't hibernate.

So this is part of the good old days for me. I loved exploring all the places on the farm that was so different from Grandma's farm. The buildings seemed newer and so much more modern.

The farmhouse where I was born, with
the barn and windmill I never saw.

The farm with the barn I milked cows in.

What deer saw when they watched
us watch them in winter.

I'm still hanging on for dear life even though
we aren't moving. Calvin is on the tractor.

Grandpa John's harvest operation. I would
love to have seen that tractor in operation.

Dad's harvest operation. Still fascinating to me.

Sometimes bundles missed the
threshing machine feeder.

Jack and Jill were white horses like the Lone
Rangers, but ride them, he couldn't.

Clair with his stripped-down Ford
Model A. That was fun to ride on.

I'm giving Marcia a ride on my new wheels.

A chimney fire required a new one to be built,
then we abandoned the house in 1957.

How far we carried water to the house and
how far Lynn ran to rescue Calvin.

7

Losses

I really didn't feel like going to school that day. The day seemed to be really off somehow, and I had strange sad feeling I couldn't explain. It was June 1954; and Marcia, Margaret, and I were attending summer Bible school.

We walked across country through our neighbor's property. They didn't mind at all a bunch of kids crossing their land because it's North Dakota, to the mighty village of Carbury because it was a lot shorter than going by the main roads. We met some other kids coming from east of Eddy's place at the corner of his property and walked with them the rest of the way. There were some tracks where the farmers drove from field to field, and we stayed on them most of the way.

It was a beautiful day, but that didn't help my feeling of funk. It was a hard day, and somehow, I made it through but felt like I didn't learn anything. We headed out across country again to go home and separated from the kids going east to their homes at the corner of Eddy's property. Suddenly, the feeling of funk I had felt all day got worse, and I didn't know whether I even wanted to go home. I just felt weird.

We got home, and I noticed that Gretchen and Harold's pickup and camper were there. As we walked up to the door, Vivian met us. Harold took Marcia and Margaret away to talk to them, and Vivian said two words, "Ma died," That's about all she could say. The fog hit me full force, and I almost passed out but somehow managed to get somewhere I could be alone to think about what I just heard. She had told some of us that she would have some surgeries and be okay, but *when they operated on her head, she would die.*

Her headaches had gotten a lot worse over the past year, and X-rays showed nothing wrong. She had lost sight in one eye, and there was swelling around the eye with other symptoms of some sort of brain trauma. So doctors said they would do exploratory surgery. The operation was a success, they said. She had a sheet tumor growing around the brain that they had successfully removed. Unfortunately, she developed a blood clot when she was in recovery. They rushed her back to surgery, but it was too late.

Mom's funeral was well attended, but I couldn't tell you who were all there. There were twelve of us kids there, but Gordon couldn't make it back from Korea for some reason known only to the military. I think Mom's siblings and parents were there from Washington state, but I wouldn't know nor know what they looked like. I don't remember ever meeting any of them, but I must have when I was really little.

We had the funeral and the graveside ceremony and were back in the meeting hall at the back of the church for a meal. I had gotten some sandwiches, cookies, and Lemonaid; and then I thought of Ingalive. I remembered her saying, "How's your-r-r *mode-ehr-r-r?*" What happened next was weird. *Wow, what is happening? Why is it so cold in here all of a sudden?* I felt like I was freezing for maybe thirty to forty seconds, and then I felt puzzled about what had just happened. I didn't think it was a normal reaction to all that had taken place, but it subsided and soon I just felt sad again.

I had lost the person who told me a few years before about the birds and the bees, and she hadn't held anything back. I knew exactly how everything happened from a desire for sex to the process of creating a new life and how the new person came into the world. Years later, I would impart that same knowledge to my son, whose only reaction was "Oooh gross!" Being fourteen years old, I needed her support to understand the weird stuff I was going through, and now she was gone. I needed to know why I was so attracted to some girls and was not really interested in others.

The change had happened so suddenly. When I was thirteen, she had been really pleased to see me talking to three girls in town when I had waited in the car for her and Dad to do some business in town (voting, I think), and they came back and saw us. She commented on how nice the girls looked. At the time, I found I liked them too, but we didn't seem to have a lot to talk about and I was feeling kind of shy. I would be attending school with them in the fall a year later. And one of them would eventually say she thought I was "stuck-up" probably because of how I acted to cover up my shyness.

In the next two months or so, many times I ran into the house to tell Mom something or ask her about something, only to stop short and realize she wasn't there and wouldn't ever be again. Why couldn't she have lived through the operation and be her old self again? I accepted the fact that she was gone and that it was for the best under the circumstances only after a weird dream.

In the dream, she had survived the operation, only she was totally unhappy. I remember in the dream, she kept saying, "I don't belong here. I need to go." Clair and I agreed to take her where she wanted to go, so she went outside and sat backward on the rear bumper of the old bodyless car that Clair had stripped. We told her she should sit on the seat, but she wouldn't. We drove to the church and stopped outside the fence next to the cemetery and started to open the gate, but she was already walking alone into the cemetery and she disappeared somewhere near where her grave is. After the dream, I knew it was what was right, and she would never have been the person I had known had she lived. Family members later told me the doctors had said she would have been a vegetable if she had lived because of all the brain damage she had sustained before and during the operation.

One day, about two months after her funeral, I was relaxing in the sun on the slanted outside basement door Dad had put up after he started digging the basement that never got finished. It made a perfect surface to lie on. It was a beautiful day, and the sun felt so good. All of a sudden, with my eyes closed, I saw the most beautiful world around me; and it was as though the universe was embracing me. I felt like I was a part of something absolutely beautiful and vast and felt love or something like I had never felt anything like before. It only lasted seconds and was suddenly gone. I wanted it back. I still want it back. Was Mom letting me know she was there? I had felt her presence so many times before, but this was totally different. Later, I questioned whether I had actually seen that beautiful sight or only imagined it from the feeling I had. I still don't know for sure how or if I "saw" it.

Mom's death had another effect on my life. I started questioning a lot of what the church taught us about God, Jesus, the afterlife, etc. I thought that when Mom went to heaven on "resurrection day," if she found any of her friends or family not there, she would actually be in hell. I've asked this question of pastors and gotten what I consider to be really stupid answers. "She would be in such ecstasy at being in heaven she would not miss them!" or "She would not remember them!" What kind of answers are those? Then, God should have created us as robots or dummies.

Suppose that a parent "loved" his child so much that he would give him great rewards if he went completely against his nature (how he was created) but if he sucked his thumb and didn't ask for forgiveness for doing so or atone for it, somehow, by the time he was one year old, he would be given to another person who would beat him every day for the rest of his life. That sort of illustrates what I thought we were to believe about God judging us for maybe eighty years of being human the way we were created and then we either go to heaven or hell *forever*! I can't accept that.

What I can believe is that we are really spirits or some other life-form inhabiting these human bodies for a short time and that the bodies we inhabit have problems and are not perfect and that we may have to inhabit several of them until we have either learned to be what we were created to be, have fixed everything we messed up, or have reached a certain level of perfection. Yes, I believe in reincarnation. I have read about—I don't remember what books—some people actually remembering previous lives and some very young children describing who they were and have talked to relatives they had in the previous life who then corroborated what they said about that life. I always say, "If you believe in incarnation of spirits, you may as well believe in reincarnation." Well, I don't really always say that, but I just did say it!

Many people are comforted by their faith, and I respect that and believe they should continue to believe what they believe. What I am writing may add to what they believe or have no impact at all. I will not try to convince anyone that they should not believe in what their church teaches; it's just that I cannot accept what most religions teach and believe. I look at this fantastic universe with all the beauty of the stars and this planet with all the fantastic life-forms we know about on it, and I can't conceive of a supreme being having created that and even having a concept of a hell to punish people forever for anything.

It could not be in such an entity's nature and also way beneath it/her/him to regard any of that creation as needing such a punishment. I can't even imagine where that concept originated, but it was human beings who originated it and wrote it into their religious books. Also, since I think we are not what we appear to be right now in this life and that maybe it would be punishing a spirit or whatever we really are for simply not being in control of the human body that we occupied (which was created with flaws anyway).

With all the stuff I had already experienced, it was hard to believe that Mom was not still nearby (I felt her presence many times) and not waiting to "rise from the dead" as the church taught. I continued attending church and ended up confirmed in the Lutheran Church even though I didn't believe much of it. I think the church teaches that even that is a sin. I actually gave what could have been called a pretty good "sermon" later on that I write about later.

I continued in the church, hoping to find better answers. The answers never came fully to my satisfaction even though I have studied books about several religions. There are around four thousand religions, five of which have large membership, and each of them is sure they have the only truth! I couldn't study all of them, of course, because life is too short; and if you asked me to tell you what those I read about believe now, I couldn't tell you much, having forgotten most of what I read. I do remember that Sadducees did not believe in life after death and maybe that is why they were *sad you see*! I had read that at least one gospel in the New Testament was written by more than one person (at least four), and someone may have added more at a later date. The clues were in the writing styles. Other books not included in the Bible have references to reincarnation.

There weren't any reporters following Jesus around writing down all the stuff he said. (He would have been misquoted in the news anyway!) It appears that most of the books of the New Testament were written centuries after his lifetime. A lot of people's memories passed on from generation to generation can be lost, misinterpreted, or corrupted in that time. I do not believe in hell, and I doubt there is a place such as purgatory.

I believe that heaven and hell are mutually exclusive for the reason I explained earlier and that you can create your own kind of hell right here on earth and maybe after death too, but that's about it. Don't get me wrong; I believe there is some truth in many of religious teachings. There were psychic people who got information about what is what in the universe but were later misinterpreted or they themselves misinterpreted the information they had received.

That information was further subverted to fit someone else's theology. But you should believe in what you believe, and I don't care what others think as long as it doesn't affect me. I will attempt to describe what I think the universe is like including what some people refer to as heaven and spirits or souls later, and maybe some of you will agree that I am somewhat on the right track. I think Jesus (yes, I believe there was such a person) was misinterpreted; was an example; and maybe not a savior because I don't believe in what we are supposed to be saved from.

I believe that he planned his own death knowing the *real him* would live on, and he did it to prove life after death in one form or another. I think that somehow that was also misinterpreted and of course distorted by those who had an agenda for making people think the way they wanted them to. Many books had been written that were not included in the New Testament, and several of them had references to reincarnation. I believe they were omitted because they didn't fit with what the early church wanted people to believe in.

If you lived several lives to make up for past indiscretions, why would you need to support the church as your only way to salvation? I think there may be several reasons why we live many lives on this earth, not necessarily just because of karma, which will one day be clear to us. We may be learning things by living many lives. I really don't understand why so many people feel so guilty for being human and think they have to be forgiven for everything unless they are really bad and did some harm to other people.

I read about Edgar Cayce and Jean Dixon and what they said about life after death and reincarnation. I found interesting some of what Edgar Cayce said about how our souls got here and why we are like we are. He appeared to have access to all records "stored" in another realm. He implied we didn't belong here, but that our souls, in experimenting with and projecting ourselves into things on this earth as well as animals, are somehow entrapped here. Now we have to find our way back out to where we belong.

Human beings were supposedly developed (through evolution maybe?) to enable that process. That along the way, we may be building up karma, thus creating the requirement to have additional "lives" (if you can call this living). Interestingly, Edgar Cayce struggled with all the stuff he said in trance because it was totally against his religion. Many books have been written about him, show that he had a very interesting life, and that he helped many people with health issues. I take solace in the fact that even Mother Teresa had questioned these things and had her doubts about some of the teachings about God and about prayer.

So I doubted most religious teaching after Mom died, but I didn't lose my curiosity about it. I started to read a lot of books about religion when I started earning enough money to buy the books. I thought about it later that I should have visited libraries, but I don't even know if we had a good one around where I lived. Later on, I did use some libraries. I do not believe prayer works for me because I am unable to do it without doubting that it works (Mom died and did not get well as a human being), so I don't try it anymore.

I believe that every thought you have in every moment of your life is equivalent to praying, and limiting thoughts limit your success in anything you attempt to do. And believe me; I ought to know. And positive thought should work the opposite. Instead of racking my brain to think of what and how to pray for what I want like I had to do each time, I think it's better to think positive thoughts as much as you can about the world and everything in it. I know that is very hard to do, especially when you see the suffering of some people and if you watch the news! When I was young, I found it very hard to think positive thoughts about myself. I was deformed after all, and in my eyes, I was ugly and stupid looking.

It may be that some future day that I will be convinced that some church is right about everything they teach, but I doubt that. But then I didn't believe in ghosts or wandering spirits either, but now that I have felt the presence of them and seen several of them, I can't deny their existence. I will explain all about this later. I have also seen family members after they had passed away but didn't realize that was what I saw until a recent event happened that convinced me they were real experiences, not just a momentary remembrance and vision of them as I remembered what they looked like.

Some more losses

Ingalive went to visit her neighbors as usual one evening in the fall when the weather was getting colder, and there was frost every night. Ole had been sick all that day, and so he had gone to bed early. She visited with Jenny for several hours, and it was getting dark out so she left to go home. After a while, Jenny turned off the yard light when she didn't see Ingalive anywhere between the houses.

Ingalive was found in the ditch, where she had fallen, the next morning, dead from exposure (at least that is what I heard happened). I shudder whenever I think of how it would feel if you fall, think maybe someone will get you up, then see the yard light go out and know that you are totally alone. It is getting cold, oh so cold, just like what I felt that day of Mom's funeral when I thought, *Wow! What is happening? Why is it so cold in here all of a sudden?*

Why can't the signals we receive be more understandable? Had I known what that was all about at the time, could I have somehow saved Ingalive? Or did her soul decide for her that was her time to go and nothing could have stopped it from happening? I probably couldn't have done a thing anyway because I lived three-and-a-half miles away. Anyway, she and Mom are probably still talking about the good old days or something wherever they are now, unless they are already occupying human bodies somewhere. But then maybe they are sisters and are talking to each other, or maybe they still communicate even if not close to each other as I speculate about later.

My high school friend Andy's father died that same year. Some thought my dad and his mom would get together, but I knew they were not at all compatible and it was never going to happen. Andy and I actually lost touch with each other after a trip to San Francisco when he and his mom stayed in California and I went back home to North Dakota because neither of us were good letter writers. I didn't have his phone number, and we just got so busy with our own stuff. I'll tell you about the San Francisco trip in the next chapter.

Not many of us left

Now there are only the three youngest girls and me still alive of the original thirteen of us that grew up to be adults. I won't be able to corroborate many childhood facts now as others' memories are not what they used to be. We have also lost three brothers-in-law and two sisters-in-law, one very recently. I and my younger sisters are still pretty good at remembering stuff, so I have to finish writing this before our brains become too forgetful. Got to keep doing sudoku and learning other stuff to keep the brains working!

Many of my former coworkers, ex-girlfriend Pat, best friend Andy, and so many others I have known are all gone to wherever we go when we pass on (which I will speculate about later). I am really curious about where that really is (but I think I know), what it is like there, what they really look like, and what they are doing there. I will, however, wait patiently for my inner being to decide when it is time to go and hope it isn't too horrible an ending. Let me look into the sky and see the meteorite just before it flattens me like a pancake! Hopefully, it will be something even less painful. Like I often say, "I don't want some strange physical or brain disorder like Seter exploding brain syndrome (SEBS) or horrible disease named after me!"

8

San Francisco

It was the summer of 1955, and a bunch of us kids had been selected to go to San Francisco to attend a Luther League Convention. We hopped on a couple of school buses and a big bus and headed for California. I got to ride in the big bus, which wasn't too bad for comfort and was a smoother ride than the other buses.

About halfway through the trip, a big guy in the seat ahead of me decided to recline his seat; and as it reclined, he gave it an extra shove, which unfortunately did not stop reclining and I found the back of his seat jammed against my knees. He had busted the seat! When asked to change places, he refused. He thought it was very funny, the @#$&@##!

Well, the buses were full, so there was no way to move anywhere else. I just put up with it for the rest of the day. It still wasn't fixed the next day, so I said I would sit there if they put a lighter person in the busted seat in front of me, which they did. Sometime later on the trip, I think they must have either fixed the seat or jammed something in it to keep it from reclining.

Andy, my best friend from high school, was one of the ones to attend the convention so we hung out together for everything: all the talks, meals, and what recreation we could find. We had rooms next to each other at the Grant Hotel. Some tours were planned for everyone, like the trip to the Muir Woods, Golden Gate Park, etc. We went to a movie presented in Cinerama, but for some reason, I can't remember what the movie was. That was when they used three projectors to put the whole thing on the screen and they weren't that well matched,   so there were obvious breaks in the scenery and everything looked like there was a hill in the middle.

San Francisco was really cool and quite clean in those days. We had a lot of fun riding the street cars, and riding in a taxi was unbelievably exciting because they must have hit forty miles per hour at times going downhills and not much slower over the top of the bumps that were cross streets. It was accelerating, decelerating, accelerating, slam on the brakes, and screech to a stop for red lights, then accelerating again. Going uphill was exciting also because you couldn't see what was ahead on the cross streets. What a ride!

The lectures were held at the Convention Center. There were several lectures to attend each day, and they were fairly generous with the lunch breaks. So we always had time to go back to our rooms to drop off notebooks, go out to get our lunch, and back to the rooms to get notebooks and head for the Convention Center for the afternoon sessions.

One day, we dropped off our notebooks and were going out to lunch when, all of a sudden, three guys from our group jumped out into the hallway and grabbed Andy and said that they were holding him hostage until I went out to buy them a bottle of wine (California Port, I think, they asked for). They were seventeen at the time and had been kicked out of the liquor store down the street.

I said, "If you guys were kicked out, how the heck will I be able to buy it?" They said that I look old for my age. So off I go to the liquor store with my knees shaking and about to panic. If I had seen a cop as I entered the liquor store, I think I would have passed out! I asked for the bottle of port. The guy hands me a bag with the wine in it and takes the money and gives me the change. I almost felt like saying, "You know I am only fifteen, so you shouldn't do this." But my worry was now if I see a cop, I will die! Well, the saga doesn't end there.

Andy and I went out to lunch at a nice cafeteria. The lighting was very low at the tables, but the smells of food were really tempting. I was really hungry, so I decided to order a piece of the great-looking roast beef that had just come out of the oven. It was a huge thing, and a lot of people were ordering it. You ordered at the beginning of the line, and by the time I got to wherever all the meat was being served, they would have it cut and on a plate. But there was a big line ahead of us, so by the time I got there, it was cut down to about half the size it started out.

It looked a little red in the middle when I got there but still looked really delicious. I got it with mashed potatoes, gravy, and some great-looking mixed vegetables. As I was eating, I thought, *Gee this is getting really cool.* I held the plate up to get a little bit closer to the light to take a closer look and found that the beef was frozen in the middle. It actually had frost on the center! We had to hurry now because we had been in the cafeteria a little too long waiting in line. I ate what I could around the edges of the meat. I had a piece of banana crème pie for dessert, and it was great. I thought nothing else could ruin the day anymore, but I was wrong.

When we got to the hotel, the three guys came out again, only this time they had opened their door and dragged us into their room as we were walking by. They were already in no shape to be seen in the halls. The wine bottle was empty, and they wanted another one. So Andy was a hostage again, and I had to make a second trip to the liquor store. Well on the way, I plotted and schemed and tried to think how I could get even. I decided to ask for a bottle of cheap wine that looked like Port but maybe had poison or something in it. I got it and delivered it, and Andy and I split really fast.

We looked at the time and decided since we seem to have missed most of this lecture, why not make it a day and go to the movies? Which we did. We saw the *Invasion of the Body Snatchers*, which was one of the first horror films I had ever seen. It gave me the willies for some time afterward, but I thought it sure did finish off a crappy day! I didn't really sleep well that night, not because of the trick I had pulled on the guys but that the movie was creepy.

What's funny about the whole thing was when I was buying the wine, I had this urge to yell at the guy at the liquor store, "Dummy, I'm only fifteen!" It probably would have solved a whole lot of problems that day, but I am glad I didn't. The three dudes didn't show their faces the next day except to grumble once about the rotten-tasting rotgut stuff I had gotten them the second time. They were in pretty bad shape with hangovers. They couldn't even drink water without getting sick again, I guess. Not only that, but they had gotten into trouble with the counselors.

To prove that no good deed goes unpunished when we got back home, we had to report on the trip in church, and each of us had to tell about some of the lectures to the congregation. Guess which lectures were assigned to me? Yep, the afternoon I missed going to the movies. I quickly borrowed notes from two of the girls who had attended, knowing they would have the best notes; copied what I could; and got ready to present my speeches by reading the notes over and over. Somehow, each time I read them, the information seemed even less clear. I was beginning to panic that I was really going to screw things up so bad that everyone would know I didn't have a clue as to what I had supposedly heard in the lectures.

The time came for me to give my presentation and I was shaking in my boots. (I really did have boots, but they were the kind of engineer boots that had a zipper in one side.) I climbed unto the pulpit and looked around at all the people waiting expectantly for words of wisdom and panicked a bit, looked at my notes, and started to introduce the date and subjects that I hoped had been covered that day. I started talking, and all of a sudden, I felt totally calm. As I finished each sentence, the next sentence was clear in my mind, and that continued for maybe ten minutes when I realized I had not looked at my notes at all throughout the presentation. Wow, what just happened? What had I said? I didn't know! Did I look like a total idiot? Maybe I should just run and hide before someone said anything. I didn't hear or I don't remember hearing any of the other presentations that followed mine.

The whole thing finished, and a couple people came up to me and asked if I planned to be a preacher when I grew up. I said, "I don't think so because I hope to be an engineer." (Not necessarily to match the boots!) I asked the girls that I got the notes from whether I had messed it up, and they said I had done a great job. Our pastor who had gone with us to the convention said I did a fine job, and I should think about going into his profession. I really do wish I could remember anything I said, but I can't. Where did the words and sentences come from, and how did they get into my head and automatically come out of my mouth? Why did I not remember anything I said? Insane rain continues!

As a clerk in a liquor store, would you sell this
guy wine without asking for ID?

9

Love Life and Beginning My Career

Okay, more weird psychic stuff ahead. I woke up one morning recently with the thought I had to write about all of this in which I will possibly be providing way too much information: some weird, some embarrassing, and some totally stupid. Although it is an important part of how I ended up married, who I married, my job, and the weird path I took to get to where I am, it may, in some horrible way, relate to an incident that occurred in Santa Barbara, California, a few years ago. I'll write more about that at the end of this chapter.

When I was about twelve, I started to notice something interesting about girls. However, I also became aware that my chest had that ugly shape I described earlier, and I was suddenly very self-conscious about it. I had had a great sense of humor up to this point, but now, life was not as funny anymore. I spent a lot of time deep breathing, trying to pop my chest into normal shape. It didn't work. I even thought about what kind of accident I could have where they would have to fix me up normal.

Not getting enough sun or not producing enough vitamin D when you are in the sun causes the bones to be soft. The doctor said cod liver oil was the way you get supplemental vitamin D in those days, so that's what I did. But taking that probably helped solidify the deformed bones just the way they were, and it tasted awful. I felt downright ugly, and that pretty much determined my relationships along with another factor I still think is unbelievable that I will hope-fully explain. Cod liver oil tastes terrible, even if flavored with mint.

My future sister-in-law and eventually sister-in-law Myra was always commenting on how I was very handsome, which I thought she did only to tease Marvin. It always seemed to work because he would make some remark about it. I never thought it was true, and I just saw what I thought was a dumb-looking person when I looked in the mirror. I was very shy and had a hard time talking to people, especially speaking in front of anyone or in a group.

I was so shy, I would blush when I talked to myself! I could usually have some conversation with another person, but if there were three of us, I became a good listener or maybe a good thinker because lots of times I found the conversations really boring! I usually had something really profound to add to a conversation about a half hour after the conversation had ended! I hated school because you had to answer questions. Don't get me wrong; I loved to learn stuff and was always studying books and encyclopedias, but it was sharing infor-mation I had trouble with.

Lots of times, I would start explaining something but cut short of fully explaining or answering something because I would skip some, mix up or run out of words, and I would feel like a fool. Even when I started conversations, they would soon die because no one seemed interested in talking to me, especially the girls, at least that's what I thought. I believed they disliked me because they thought I was dumb looking or maybe even ugly because I felt that way. By the time this part of the book is done, I may wish I had run out of words!

When I was twelve years old and attending grade school, with first through eighth grades in a one-room school, I had started to be interested in the opposite sex. In the fifties, the girls all wore the skirts that were below the knee, and they wore them all year long when they were out in the public, even in the winter, wearing slacks under them when it was very cold and they were going outside.

When they came into the schoolhouse, they would remove the slacks out in the hall. One girl, I will call her Em, would then stand over the heat register with her skirt billowing out enough to reveal maybe two inches of thigh above the knees. I found this to be extremely attractive for reasons I could not at all understand at the time. It was very confusing, these new feelings about her. The feelings got a real kick-start when, one day,   the girls had forgotten to close the door to the hall before they removed the slacks.

I had a slight cold that day and had stayed in during recess, trying to get rid of a headache. I was facing the door with my head down on my arms on the desk, trying to relax the headache away with my eyes closed. Hearing the girls talking, I opened my eyes just in time to see Em hiking up her skirt and adjusting whatever she had on under it. I saw her from the side, but that was enough to give me a view of the entire length of her leg and her shape under her panties. My reaction in a certain area was immediate and surprised me because it was the first time my physical reaction had ever happened.

Even though Mom had told me it would happen, it was very sudden and unexpected. When I thought about it later, I had the same reaction. Hormones were raging! What is weird about this is I felt embarrassed, exhilarated, guilty, and sad all at the same time. Even though I am sure she didn't know I had witnessed the whole thing, I felt guilty for having witnessed what could have been very embarrassing to her if she was as modest as my sisters seemed to be. But I loved it! I couldn't help it.

It was so confusing since the year before that, I wasn't really interested in girls. It made me sad because I was so shy, I didn't even know how to talk to girls much less have relationships with them like the older boys had been doing the year before. Girls must be attracted to guys earlier than guys are to girls because the girls had been messing around (no, not that way) with the older boys long before I got interested in the girls.

One time toward the end of the school year when I was in the eighth grade (Em was in seventh grade) I got really brave and I hinted I wanted to get together with her at recess for maybe a hug or whatever we were brave enough to do. The time was approaching, but something else was happening also—an urge to go to the outhouse (yes, we had them at our school too) that was actually starting to hurt and burn a little.

At recess, I headed out as fast as I could, still hoping to get that job done and then meet her for maybe a few minutes at least. I couldn't seem to stop whatever was being expelled from my backside, so I used some toilet paper to see whatever was ailing me. OMG, I was bleeding back there. The day before, I had had a really hard time literally, and today it was my first—butt not last—hemorrhoid experience. I didn't know what it was, and I was bleeding to death as far as I knew. It finally stopped, but I was actually a couple minutes late getting back to class and very late as far as any type of relationship with Em.

She wouldn't let me explain what happened, and she made her hatred for me known for the remaining six weeks of school. If this had not happened, what would my life have been now? Quite different, I suspect, but my life seems to have been directed in one direction by something or some entity I carry around with me. That one experience affected all my relationships from then on because I thought girls could never forgive even one booboo! Even though North Dakota is an almost unpopulated state, I never saw her again, and we lived only about four miles from each other.

This may seem to be way off the subject, but it is important to facts I will reveal later. Whenever I was reading stuff in the *D* encyclopedia in grade school, I invariably found myself looking at a picture of a dog called a toy terrier. I hated dogs, having been bitten by a few of the neighbor dogs. We had had a dog when I was a toddler and a few years later, but he was very old and crippled with arthritis so we couldn't play with him anyway. Hating dogs, I wondered why I liked the one in the encyclopedia. It was downright cute and seemed to be a perfect small dog. No other dog in the encyclopedia got my attention at all. I thought if I ever had a dog, it would be one like that.

I started high school and soon found I had a friend named Andy (a nickname not anything like his real name) who, I mentioned before, had the same interests I had. He is the one with me in San Francisco that was held for ransom for wine! We both were interested in science and science fiction, and we were also interested in space travel and what it would take to get to the moon and maybe the planets.

I don't know if he was into the dating scene at all because we never discussed that. I suspect he may have had a few dates though. I was still as shy as ever though and really self-conscious about my deformity and wanted something that could take my mind off my problems. I thought maybe basketball would be a fun sport and maybe even make girls more interested, so I joined the basketball team.

Andy was also in it, so I thought that would make it even better. There, I was learning to do layups, dribble the ball, and shoot from various places on the court. It was lots of fun the first two practices, and I was finally enjoying some sort of sport for a change even though I thought I wasn't good at it. Also, we got to see the cheerleader practice. Third practice, the coach decided we were going to have a scrimmage game, so he separated us into two groups and assigned the two groups the titles shirts and skins. Shirts play with shirts on, skins play with no shirts. I was assigned to the skins team, which meant I had to play with my chest bare and visible to the whole school.

I did it and survived some stares and made it through, but I dropped out of basketball that day. There was no way I was going to go through that again. Andy thought joking about it may make me feel better; so when he saw me later, he said "Holey, holey, holey," like the religious song. I did laugh, but it really didn't help much. It didn't help either that I was one of those ninety-seven-pound weaklings like in the stupid ad put out by Joe Weider for bodybuilding.

Basically, in the cartoon ad, the big guy takes the girl away from the ninety-seven-pound weakling on the beach after he makes fun of the weakling and knocks him down. There were several different ads that had slightly different scenarios, and some of them can still be found on the internet. The weakling then takes Joe's course in bodybuilding, and in the one I remember, he wins the girl back by knocking out the big dude. I question why you would want the girl back after she left with the muscleman! Anyway, I was skinny as a rail besides having the messed-up chest. It didn't help any that I had heard one girl say that I was stuck-up. I may have appeared that way to her only because I was so shy.

My problems talking in a group really bothered me during high school, at least the two years I actually attended a real high school. One day in science class, the teacher asked me to explain some scientific reason for some phenomena like moon phases as an example. This was my time to shine on a subject I had down pat, and maybe I could actually impress someone with my knowledge. Okay, so I may have done a pretty good job of explaining how both the moon and inner planets go through phases. (I think that may have been the subject but now am not sure because that seems too simple, but you get the point.) And I was proud!

The teacher said, "Now explain it so the rest of us can understand it!" Then, he called on someone else. There were many other instances like this, but like I said, the actual subjects are hazy now. One time, I heard some of the guys and girls talking in one of the classrooms, but I don't remember now what they were talking about. I heard some of the conversation before I opened the door to go in there and thought of a really funny response to what I heard. I opened the door, walked in, and said it while trying my hardest to stifle my own laughter. And I did manage to say it with a straight face.

Blank stares, both male and female, is the only response I got from my hilarious contribution to the conversation. After a few seconds of total silence, I turned and walked out the door, and as I left, I heard one of the guys say the exact words I had just spoken followed by roaring laughter. I loved to learn, but I hated high school, at least at that school at that moment!

When I was sixteen and got my driver's license, I got real brave thinking I may attempt dating, which is what most guys seemed to be doing. There was one girl in particular that I thought was the most beautiful one in the world. I went into Bottineau, thinking if I learn to roller-skate, I would be able to meet girls because they all seem to spend a lot of time at the roller-skating rink. As soon as I walked in, I saw her. What a coincidence that was.

She was coming off the rink and was just sitting down to change into her regular shoes. She was with three other girls who had already changed and were waiting about thirty feet away. I had actually spoken to her one time outside the movie theater. When she dropped something, I had picked it up to give it back to her, and we had introduced ourselves to each other. Wow, what luck if I could just conjure up enough courage to ask her for a date.

Shaking in my boots, I went up to her and asked if she had been skating long that day, and she said only about an hour. She had her shoes changed and started to get up when I thought it is now or never. I said, "If you aren't busy next Saturday night..." I didn't get any further than that because she looked at me with what I interpreted as horror or maybe deer-in-headlights look, turned, and walked toward her friends.

The lump I had in my throat felt like I had tried to swallow a baseball. I saw them looking at me after she said something to them as I left the building still shivering from the experience. I never learned to roller-skate. I also didn't ask anyone for dates for some time after this. After that, I went to a store that sold magazines and bought a couple of joke books that had pictures of pinup ladies in them. They didn't help! How did a sixteen-year-old buy adult magazines and books? I looked old for my age as I had found out on the trip to San Francisco. I remember many people I grew up with or even some I met briefly, but for some reason, I cannot recall her name. It's as though her name was erased from my memory or that I had never even known it.

A couple of weeks went by, in which I had time to really feel sorry for myself and think what an ugly mess I must be, so I was really in a bad mood when a phone call came in that was for me. A female voice on the other end of the line asked if I would be willing to go on a blind date. I had no idea whether it was a young girl or somebody's mom on the phone. I answered, "I can't," and hung up the phone. I simply didn't feel worthy of any body's affection. I also thought for the first time about suicide, but then I said to myself, *I can't.*

Some months later, Clair, Calvin, and I went to visit a friend who had returned from the Army. We parked in front of the house where he lived with about five siblings. Clair, Calvin, and the friend all sat in the front seat of the car, telling jokes, talked what they had done in the Army, and about all kinds of fun they had had while I sat in the back seat, listening to all the juicy and funny stuff. I thought it was a bit strange that they chose to sit crowded in front, but I had fun listening to them talking anyway.

Suddenly, his little sister (my age) showed up dressed in a somewhat short dress with high heels and nylons and with lots of makeup and opened the back door, climbed in, and proceeded to slide across the seat and hoisted herself onto my lap. She made no attempt to pull her dress down, which was hiked up to where thigh was showing above her nylons, which were held up with garters.

These days, short dresses are everywhere but not in those days, so this was quite exciting. My reaction was as immediate as the incident with Em in grade school but a lot more intense. I was overwhelmed by what I saw and felt and was ready to let her do whatever she wanted to do. In the years I hadn't seen her since about fourth or fifth grade in school, she had changed into a very attractive, well-endowed young girl.

I was thrilled that, all of a sudden, someone of the opposite sex was showing that much interest in me. I was a little shy but really wanted what I thought was about to happen, but in a moment, that all changed. Suddenly, I was panicked because I knew something else—I didn't know what—was going on that I should be very concerned about. I thought, *What is happening is all wrong. It cannot happen, and I have to stop it.*

I closed my eyes and told her to get off my lap. I said it several times, and finally, she got disgusted and got out of the car. She proceeded to climb in the front seat and sat on Calvin's lap, and so now there are four people in front. Every once in a while, she would sneak a peek over his shoulder, I assume to see what effect it had on me, and I tried to ignore it as much as possible. I wondered how she could be such a tease right next to her big brother.

I felt somewhat stupid, sad, confused about my feelings, and a little mad at Calvin but, weirdly, relieved. Eventually, Calvin walked her to the house and returned to join the conversation again. Just before he got in the car, he grinned at me, and I don't know whether he was approving of what I had done or thought it was pathetic. I never asked what he thought, nor did I care. I just knew that somehow, I had escaped some kind of problem but didn't have a clue as to what it was. A few months later, I heard she had gotten married and she must have been pregnant at the time of this event.

I only attended an actual high school during my freshman year and junior year. Because Dad didn't want me driving to school after a drunk forced me off the road one rainy morning, he decided that I would take those two years through correspondence courses (by mail). I don't know if I explained to him satisfactorily what had really happened that day. We were both driving black Chevy pickup trucks. I had just crossed a bridge, and the guy just kept coming toward me. I kept moving toward the right side of the road, and when he passed me going the opposite direction, our outside rearview mirrors actually hit each other.

I tried to get back off the muddy shoulder of the road, but it was too late because the back wheel slipped off the road and the pickup started to tilt into the ditch. I just turned into the ditch to keep from rolling. I stayed with my sister Gretchen and Harold in Anaconda, Montana, for my junior year. I think one year of me was enough for them.

Just before I left to go back home in North Dakota at the end of the school year, a friend and his girlfriend got me to go on a blind date with her friend, which was nice because we actually talked and I got my first good-night kiss. I was seventeen at the time. We didn't date after that because she lived over 750 miles away. Besides, I was still too shy to ask anybody else. Fear of rejection and shyness were strong in this one! I apologize, but I had to work in a Star Wars-like phrase somehow, at least once in this thing I'm calling a book.

Shortly after, I got back from Montana, when we moved off the farm into the huge city of Carbury, population maybe ten; and we lived in the back of the post office where sister Vivian was the postmistress. She kept telling me I should ask SS for a date. Heck, I had tried talking to her several times, and we never got more than a couple of sentences before the conversation died.

I would rack my brains trying to think of topics that may interest her and always ended up blank. After I turned eighteen, we were both attending the community college in Bottineau, and somehow, I ended up driving us both to school. When she got into the car, she sat in the back seat like I was her chauffer or something. That is not conducive to me asking her for a date at all. I figured she probably had a boyfriend, and seeing us together in front was probably not what she wanted so I never asked her for a date.

Sometimes, she talked me into driving her and several of her girlfriends to the Dairy Queen, and that's where the next part happened. Her friends were pretty, cute, and very attractive; but I found it as hard to talk to them as to her. Conversations always seemed to end quickly. They didn't attempt to keep them going, and I just felt dumb because I would run out of things to talk about.

I had seen a girl in shorts at Dairy Queen, and I can only describe what I saw as having Betty Grable legs so I will call her BGL. If you saw pinup calendars from around that time, you would know what I mean. They were nice. It turns out BGL was my sister Marcia's friend at the time, and she was sixteen. I was twenty when I asked her for a date. She accepted, and we went to the movies.

We had a few dates, and for some time, everything seemed okay. But there was that nagging thought in the back of my mind about how I would mention that my physical shape is weird without freaking her out or something. How do I tell her that if she ever wanted to go swimming or some such thing that I would never do that? I knew she liked to go to the Friday-night dances, and I had never learned to dance and never intended to.

I found that I really was not that into her as a girlfriend because we didn't seem to have any interests in common, and my eyes were beginning to wander and I found some others were attracting me more. I was getting ready to move to a real city to go to college. Now that I think about it, we didn't talk that much either. It was still hard to carry on a conversation even on a date, so it's a good thing no one talked during movies.

The problem, if you can call it that, was solved by my sister-in-law Myra when she set me up with a date with her cousin, whom I will call CG for cute girl. I don't know why I thought she had arranged it with Myra, but that was my impression of how it all happened. So I took her to the movie in Bottineau, which now that I think about it was my inner being scheming again. I had thought about taking her to Minot to the movies but didn't.

To make a long story really short, BGL saw us there, and the date BGL and I had later on lasted maybe a minute and a half before she told me exactly what she thought of CG and me and that I should take her back home. I did feel guilty about having this happen to Marcia's friend; but in a way, it made it easier to just leave to attend UND, Grand Forks, that fall. But I would still have to figure out what to tell CG about my leaving to go to college.

I had promised a guy that he could ride with me to Grand Forks because all he had was a motorcycle which he didn't want to take to college, and he lived near the town where CG and Myra's parents lived. He wanted me to meet him at a bar in town, and he would show me how to get to his place, which was not easy to describe. None of the roads had numbers or any identification of any kind in those days (now they are numbered county roads), so it would have been impossible for me to find otherwise.

It was Friday night, and of course, there was a dance happening that night so the town was busier than usual. I saw CG going to the dance, so I told her I needed to talk to her about something but had to wait at the bar for someone first. The guy never showed up, and I waited maybe an hour and a half. Went to the dance hall, but CG wouldn't talk to me. She just made an anguished sound when I asked to go somewhere we could talk.

All I wanted to do was to tell her I was going to college and wanted to know if we should continue dating whenever I was home or if we should just call it quits. On my way out, I saw BGL was there. I should have known she would be there, and she probably had a confrontation with CG. I'm off to college and now have no ties to anyone.

As shy as I still was, I didn't date any college girls. I probably couldn't have afforded to anyway because I had to get loans to go to school, and I borrowed from family members too. Besides, I was in a tough curriculum that required lots of studying. I planned to be an electrical engineer. Besides that, I still could not carry on a conversation with girls. It was impossible.

They didn't seem to want to talk to me. It was weird because the ones I had dated seemed to be able to keep a conversation going at least for a little while. I had pretty much accepted the fact that I would probably end up being a bachelor like so many of our neighbors were. Our next-door neighbor Eddy was a bachelor as was his neighbor on the farm to the south of his, and there were three brothers that lived between our place and great city of Carbury along SR-14. All three, I believe, had never been married. Yep, that was to be my fate; I was sure.

I got a summer job so I could earn enough to at least pay for some of the college expenses. I worked with a utility crew; and our work was mostly outside putting up power poles, building or updating equipment in power substations, and fixing power distribution lines. Another college student working at the same place and I got rooms in the basement of a hotel. It was cheap, probably because the rooms were dark and dingy down there. They were pretty crummy rooms, but for starving college students, they were okay.

One night, I dreamed I was driving along a highway that had high cliffs on the left side and a huge body of water on the right. There were large waves breaking on the shoreline that in places was right next to the highway. I was thinking about where we should explore after my wife, Gloria, got off work. I woke up remembering that much of the dream.

What a weird dream since I was not married and had no idea what she may look like if I had a wife and had no clue where I was. I puzzled over the dream, wondering if maybe I would live somewhere in Minnesota or Michigan and somewhere by the Great Lakes, and I didn't know what kind of job I had. None of that was in the dream. Where she worked was not in the dream. Or was it all there and I didn't remember any of that?

Then it dawned on me. There was a very pretty girl who worked at the café named Gloria. Could she be the one? I thought about it all day at work and was getting pretty excited about it by the end of the day. What would I say to her? After work, I took a shower and got all shiny and shaved again. I put on lots of Old Spice aftershave and headed to the café, thinking I'll get supper there and figure out how to ask for a date.

The first thing I saw as I walked in the door was that Gloria was crying. One of the work crew was coming toward the door, obviously angry; and as he walked out and just before he slammed the door, he yelled, "Damned lesbian!" Shocked, I stopped in my tracks momentarily, then realizing what just happened, I made a U-turn and went out the door. I was also shocked at my reaction. I was mad! I felt like following him and giving him a swift kick in the butt.

Why would anyone treat a pretty girl like that? Of course, I didn't do a thing because I knew he was a lot bigger and stronger than I was, and it wouldn't have been a pretty sight: me, the ninety-seven-pound weakling against him, the He-Man. Joe would not have been any help to me, my being a farm kid who could never build muscle beyond what I had. Not enough testosterone, I guess, and even though I carried two five-gallon buckets of water, I would never have the muscle that guy had.

I realized, obviously, that's not my Gloria. It was really weird how I thought about her though, having mixed feelings of being sorry for her, knowing she liked girls more than guys but knowing somehow it was okay. I liked girls much better than guys too, and it was okay for me. But I felt they didn't like me back!

I didn't like some guys at all because they seemed so sure they were God's gift to the world or something, and some of them seemed absolutely stupid! I felt like guys didn't trust me either, and I could not imagine what that was all about. Some of the guys seemed to treat girls badly, and yet the girls seemed to adore them! Insane! That's just how I felt about it. Insane rain falling everywhere! That dream was just crazy! By now, I was really sure I was to be a bachelor.

I got back to the hotel later after I found another place to have supper, as we called it then. I walked in and sat down in the waiting room and started looking at some of the brochures for things to do around town or maybe go check out the great city of Minot and see if there was something I might be interested in attending when, all of a sudden, I feel hands rubbing my shoulders and going into the back of my shirt. It is the hotel manager, and OMG, he is making a pass at me.

The things he was saying implied that women couldn't compare to what men could do. I just pulled away and said, "Leave me alone. I'm not what you think I am." I went to my room disgusted about what had just happened. Needless to say, this was a bit too much to have happen in one day, and I felt really weirded out about it all.

During my senior year in college, I met another friend of Marcia's, Pat, a real cute girl with a great sense of humor. We dated some whenever I wasn't working on weekends or in college almost two hundred miles away. We actually could carry on a conversation for more than two sentences, and we seemed to like each other. She was studying to be a nurse, so I had confided in her the feelings I had about my ugly chest because I thought of all people she would understand. And in return, she told me she had a spare tire that never went flat! I thought it was a cute way of saying, "I'm a little bit plumper than I would like to be." It didn't matter to either of us that the other one wasn't perfect because we seemed to be connecting in other ways.

After college, I had a job lined up in California working for the Navy as electronics engineer at a place called Point Mugu Naval Air Station where aircraft and missile systems were tested. Employees that worked there had come to recruit employees at UND. I would be on probation, meaning I could be fired easily, for a year and going through what they called the junior professional (JP) program. I would work in three different departments while the Navy evaluated my performance.

I suspect I had already been investigated for a security clearance starting as soon as I had filled out an application for employment before I finished college because I had my clearance almost immediately. Pat and I decided that we would say goodbye for then or forever and I would move to California, but we decided we would still stay in touch through the mail and periodically by phone.

My first JP tour was in the Electronic Devices Division of the Range Development Department, but I wasn't succeeding in getting anything done so I almost flunked out of the program. Part of the problem was I knew a lot about designing electronics with vacuum tubes, but the first job I had was troubleshooting circuits designed with brand-new devices called transistors. I had no knowledge of how they worked, and I didn't have a working model to compare with so I had to research how they worked and discovered that all the literature on the subject was almost impossible to comprehend.

Anyone who knew how the things and the devices built with them were supposed to operate was on travel out on the test range and were not expected to be around for several weeks if they were lucky, for months if not. I found out that even though I was homesick a little and kind of hated California and was already starting to hate my job because of that first assignment, the biggest problem was I missed Pat tremendously. I told her I wish I could do it in person, but I was asking her to marry me on the phone and she said yes.

I said I'll send a cheap engagement ring as a placeholder for now and plan to get a better one later after we see each other again to be sure we both were serious. Maybe we will wait two years until she graduates from nursing school to finalize plans. I felt better, but now I didn't have much more time to improve my performance on the first JP tour. And I still didn't understand transistors, having burned out several of them trying out circuit designs to see how they worked.

I started my second JP tour in the Flight Test Division in the Weapons Test Department. (Note that I may not have all names correct because they kept changing every few years because if something is working well, you reorganize.) I found out I was very interested in how aircraft functioned, so I really got into it. That was the group who planned each flight test, supported the test, and analyzed the data from the test flights.

I went through aircraft maintenance manuals and created a functional block diagram of the radar and weapons fire control system of the F-4 Phantom fighter jet. That task and a few other minor tasks pretty much used up those four months, and I was amazed at how fast it went. I was starting to find my job very interesting when that tour came to an end. I thought after my next tour, I would return to Flight Test. I would have another four-month tour to complete, then I would take some time off and see Pat again and my family of course.

The JP administrator let me break the JP rules and I started my third tour in the Instrumentation Division in the same department that Flight Test was in. Tours were supposed to be in different departments, but this was a fairly new division that was building their workforce so he let me do it. The people in Instrumentation Division were designing and building telemetry systems and equipment to test aircraft and missiles.

My career was saved and redirected by a man named Ted in the Instrumentation Division who spent thirty minutes teaching me how transistors worked. He said to ignore all the garbage equations written about them; look at the specifications in the transistor manuals for transistor configuration, maximum voltage, and current specifications; and ignore the rest of it. He then drew several sample circuits for each of the two transistor configurations and told me how they worked. I was now a transistor circuit designer and blew up very few of them from then on.

They were simpler than vacuum tubes for sure because for vacuum tubes, you had to use the charts, graphs, and data to calculate load and bias resistor values and they used gobs of power. When my tour there ended, he talked me into staying in the division because it was hands-on hardware work that would never be boring like flight test paperwork would end up being. I think he saw more potential in me than I did.

I found out my F-4 aircraft block diagram was actually being used by several guys in different departments to help with analyzing problems that came up now and then in the F-4 aircraft. That was a source of some pride for me in my own work, even though I still had doubts about my capabilities and I really felt inferior to other engineers who seemed to know so much more than I did. Later, I found out some of the engineers had had summer jobs at Point Mugu while they were in school under the Student Education Development (SED) program. No wonder they had a head start on me. If I had done that, it would have been a long commute from North Dakota!

Pat and I were together again with me on vacation in North Dakota, but this time, it felt a bit different to me. Maybe because I thought we would be married someday and it scared me a bit, but

I really couldn't put my finger on exactly what was going on about my mixed feelings. I told her I would check into colleges near my work where she could finish nurse's training, but I didn't think she responded well to that.

To make a long story shorter, after I returned to California, my sister informed me that Pat almost messed up and wore the wrong ring while I was with her. She apparently had two other engagement rings and was dating both guys. It must have been a real shuffling match to make sure she had the right one on. Don't know how that worked out for her except I do know her marriage to one guy didn't last long at all.

A friend introduced his sister-in-law to me when she came to visit from out of state. We spent a lot of time together and really seemed to be meant to be together. She was beautiful. I thought she was perfect, and I was in love. We even talked about getting married at one point. She left to go back home, and I looked forward to making plans together. My friend asked me to come over to his house a few weeks later; and there, I met her father, who immediately asked me if we planned to get married.

Suddenly, it dawned on me I had never spoken to her about my physical condition, my caved-in chest, and thought about what a wedding night surprise that would be. I thought about all the other guys she probably had to choose from. Suddenly, I felt totally inadequate and unworthy of her, so I was hesitant to give a yes-or-no answer right on the spot. In fact, I don't remember what I said, but it was not a good answer.

To make a long story short, about two weeks after her father went back home, I got the Dear John letter from her with regrets it couldn't work out. I speculate later how I may have screwed this up on purpose (something's purpose) by not mentioning my chest. I vowed that if I was ever in a similar situation in the future, one of the first things about me to get mentioned was that. But I really didn't think it would ever happen again and I was to be a bachelor for sure.

In California, no one asks if you are married; they ask if you've *been married*. Many have been but are no longer unless they are on spouse number X. I still found I could not get the ladies to talk to me, but I did have a few friends. One of them talked me into moving from Oxnard to Santa Monica. He said traffic was better that way, and Santa Monica was "where the action is." I stayed in his apartment with him and another of his friends while my apartment was being vacated by the old tenants, cleaned, and painted.

I slept in my blankets on the floor as did his other temporary guest. One morning, he asked me, "Who is Gloria?"

I said, "I don't know."

He said, "You talked about her in your sleep."

I racked my brains trying to figure out which of the women—I had met two Gloria's, but they were both married—I would have been talking about. They were both pretty, and they had both flirted with me. I discovered that married women whose husbands were away from home (Navy, etc.) didn't hesitate to flirt with me. No way was I going to mess around with a married woman, though, as I guess I took Mom's warnings about when it was okay seriously and that was if you were married.

I had asked a few single women for dates, and some had excuses like they were actually engaged and didn't wear a ring because of their job with some saying they had just broken up with a boyfriend and weren't ready to date again. But one of them really floored me when she said, "I'm not ready to settle down yet!" That caused me to pause and say to myself, *What the hell did I just ask her?* I don't remember asking her to marry me or anything like that.

Yes, I know I used that word for a place I don't believe in, but it seems to fit so well as an expletive for what had just happened. Norwegians normally all say, "Uff da," in situations like this; so I guess I could have said that. When I did get a date with someone, we didn't seem to communicate for long because it was the old can't-carry-on-a-conversation thing. One told me she needed to date people in the entertainment industry for her career to blossom or some such thing, and I couldn't help her with that. I don't know how that worked out for her because I never saw a movie, any stage performance, or anything with her advertised in them unless she is really famous now, has a stage name, and had a face change!

I had wanted to try the food at a restaurant called The Islander on La Cienega Boulevard in Hollywood, but I didn't want to do it alone. There was a girl in the apartment building where I lived that was going into the Navy soon, so I thought she would enjoy an exotic meal and I asked her to go with me just for dinner. She accepted; and we went and had some exotic drinks, roast duck, and over all a fantastic meal but hardly had any conversation again even though I asked her what she planned to do in the Navy and about her father who was an admiral in the Navy. I got almost nothing conversationally.

The food was fantastic, the conversation lousy. We ate and returned to our apartments. I thanked her for going with me and went back to my humdrum existence building a Heathkit transistor stereo AM/FM receiver and a vacuum tube amplifier system. I mean literally building with parts in kits, soldering components onto the circuit boards, soldering in all the wires, etc. That was the most exciting thing I was doing besides designing stuff at work. I did mess up that night though because I didn't notice I had soldered an input power resister to a ground terminal instead of the terminal next to it where it was supposed to go in the amplifier system.

I guess I was thinking too much about another failed conversation with the opposite sex. When I eventually finished building it and turned on the power, that resistor went up in smoke. The one I replaced it with had uninsulated metal caps on the ends where the leads were connected. I foolishly touched it with the power on to see if it was getting hot and accidently touched the metal chassis with my wrist. Four hundred volts DC gets your attention fast. It tends to attract whatever touches it, it really is hard to let go, and I partially lifted the amplifier off the table as I pulled away. Thankfully, it did no damage to the amplifier or to me except to make me feel very foolish. Electronic engineers are supposed to be smarter than that!

By the way, traffic was a lot better from Santa Monica because the heavy traffic was always going the other way, but I wasn't seeing any of the action! In fact, one time I was in an adult bookstore checking out magazines when a certain type of lady was approaching all the men with a proposition. Thinking I would learn something from her, I waited for her to approach, but it never happened. She had looked my way several times as she approached every other man in the place but never came near me. I'm thinking, *Uff da. I can't even attract a prostitute! I didn't even need two hands to count the number of women I have dated so far.* I could have gotten by with nine-and-a-half fingers; but thanks anyway, Mom, for letting me keep ten!

At about this same time, a really unexpected event occurred when I visited another bookstore. Andy from back in high school and the trip to San Francisco was at the same store at the same time in the middle of Los Angeles, which seems to be a one-in-a-million chance. We spent more time together, exploring some of California, and talked over old times in North Dakota, which we both missed.

I'm not sure why he hadn't gotten a college degree because he and I had about the same amount of brain power and would have both been valedictorians graduating from high school. I was. I don't know if he was because he finished high school in California, and I never thought to ask. He had a job as a bouncer at a topless bar in LA, which surprised me some because he wasn't a big dude. But back to the topic.

I'm skipping some other psychic happenings just to keep this story on track. I will get to them later. After about five years working in California, I was doing well on the job. I loved my job and had decided I liked California mostly for the weather, not the traffic. I took to the road to go on vacation in North Dakota and had a good time visiting my brother Clair in Colorado where he was a schoolteacher.

He and his wife decided we should go out and have a few drinks at a nice hotel bar in town, but she wanted to introduce me to a friend who attended the Lutheran Church they went to. The friend had to be talked into it, but she finally agreed so we went to her house where she lived with her parents. As we walked into the house, I saw a little dog, a toy terrier-chihuahua mix, then I met Gloria and her parents.

The dog just came over and sniffed me, but I didn't attempt to pet it or anything, thinking it may take my hand off. It was Gloria's dog, a spayed female, and it brought back memories of the *D* encyclopedia because it looked exactly like the dog that I had seen so many times before in grade school. Gloria later confided in me that her dog hated all men, but that her dog had accepted me right away, which she thought was some sort of omen. We talked about stuff, lots of stuff. We communicated, and even after I was back in California, we talked on the phone. We had to get married because my phone bill was six hundred dollars!

I think I would have fallen in love with her voice even if I had never seen her. She was a telephone operator and had a great voice for that. We got married the same year. I was twenty-seven, she was twenty-four, and we were both inexperienced when we got married. Of course, she knows that I like to look at and admire other women, but she is okay with it because we have an agreement: I can look but not touch. And I told her that if I stop looking, she knows to make the funeral arrangements.

She said if I did touch, she would certainly arrange a funeral! Andy flew to Colorado and attended our wedding. We moved into my apartment in Santa Monica, which would be a temporary home because we knew we wanted to buy a house one day. Gloria had said she always wanted a brother, and I gave her seven brothers-in-law and five sisters-in-law. Soon after we were married, she got nieces and nephews totaling thirty-two.

One Friday evening, it happened just as I had dreamed it. I'm driving home on the coast route California SR-1 with cliffs on the left side and the Pacific Ocean on the right, and I'm thinking about where we are going to go explore after Gloria gets off work at the bakery where she worked. We did a lot of exploring all over Southern California after work and on weekends after she got off work.

It took three years before we had children, but we have two great kids and now have four grandchildren, two of which are adults. Wow has time seemed to fly. We have had our ups and downs and she has had many medical problems, but we've hung in there for fifty-three years so far. We still talk now, but we really don't communicate very well anymore! But we are in it "till death do us part" no matter what, and I still look but I have never touched just as we had agreed a long time ago. And she hasn't had to make funeral arrangements.

Because I had no real conversations with the ladies and had no experience, I was attracted to what I saw much earlier in my life in the calendars Dad was selling and then the racier ones later. I substituted that for normal relationships with the few exceptions when I actually dated for a while, and it also filled in lonely times when Gloria was ill, which was a lot of the time after we had our second child. Gloria suffers from fibromyalgia, arthritis, and migraine headaches and has had about twenty-seven surgeries on various parts of her body. I tell her even though she isn't silly, she is a real cutup anyway. The magazines are a lousy substitute for a real relationship though.

What the heck was the problem all those years? When I was about forty or so, my sister told me that so many of the girls I had known in North Dakota asked about me and that one of them had said, "He could have had any girl he wanted, but he made them shy!" *Now that is crazy, and I find it really hard to believe. I WAS THE ONE WHO WAS SHY!*

But I've also heard from friends on several occasions, "She has the hots for you" or "she has a crush on you." But one friend told me a woman he worked with, who had been married and divorced, said to him, "He is the only man I ever met that I don't know what to say to!" That is really unbelievable, and I didn't have a clue how to respond to that. I had my deformed chest, never felt I was good-looking in any way all my life and in fact felt ugly and too skinny when I was young and too fat when I got older. When I look at pictures of myself at various ages, I still don't see it. Insane rain continues to fall!

So what connection is there with the University of California, Santa Barbara? A student in Santa Barbara shot and killed some other students before he took his own life. It was discovered later on social media that he felt that no one liked him. He had written about being lonely because he had no good friends, and he didn't date and girls didn't seem interested in him. When I saw a picture of him on TV, I thought he looked very *handsome*, a good-looking guy. *Wow!* That is what Myra said about me. Did he have the same problem with relationships that I had all those years because of how he looked and was probably shy as well? Maybe we never smiled or something. Could we have done anything or acted in any way to change our relationship to others? I'll probably never know.

When I was young, I thought that I had very few friends and was really upset about my lonely life. I had thought about suicide a few times but never attempted or thought of really attempting it. It would have been so easy with all the dangerous stuff we had on our farm. But I couldn't have done that anyway, nor could I have harmed anyone else because of it.

Now I am old, look old, have all the aches and pains of being old, and still have a caved-in sternum; but it doesn't matter what people think of me now. At least that's what I tell myself anyway. My whole life has been totally my doing and I should have tried harder to find fun in it, but I chose to see the darker side when I was young. Or maybe I have a different idea of who or what was really running the show all this time. You just have to read on to see what conclusions I make.

After I wrote this, I thought maybe it wasn't necessary—that I have written way too much information and it wasn't any bodies business. Then, I thought about the psychic part of it; and that seemed to be important enough to keep it all in: the fact that both Gloria and I never expected to ever get married, the dog, the dreams, and all the background experiences that seemed to direct everything I did seemed important. So here it is. Pathetically, it is the biggest chapter in this mess I call a book. It is also relevant to some conclusions I make later, which may explain a lot about why my life went in the direction it has.

10

Adventures in Driving and Walking

I got my license to drive when I was sixteen, and I thought I was a good driver. But Dad was concerned about how I had a tendency to move far to the right whenever I met a car going the opposite direction on two-lane roads. Of course, we had nothing but two-lane roads in our area. I thought as long as I was not driving in the ditch, it must be okay.

With my newfound freedom to travel, I had driven to the area around the towns of Newburg and Maxbass, done some exploring, and was on my way home going east on ND Highway 5. It was just getting dark when I was getting close to the Souris River crossing where there was a fairly narrow two-lane steel girder bridge across a narrow part of the river. I saw a truck coming down into the river valley from the east approaching the bridge, but it was far enough away I would be across the bridge long before I had to pass the truck.

Then, I saw a bright fireball in the north that left a long bright trail that sort of caused me to forget anything else was happening, and I had slowed considerably during the spectacle. The meteor broke up into a few pieces that each left a trail, and I wondered if one of them actually hit the ground because it looked quite low in the sky. Suddenly, I realized I was almost on the bridge, about to pass the truck, and because I had been distracted and slowed down, we were going to pass on the bridge inside that narrow structure.

If you have seen the old railroad bridges with the steel girders on the sides and over the top, you'll know what I was facing at that moment. I panicked momentarily, but then everything turned black. It got very quiet, and a voice I didn't recognize at the time commanded, "Don't move!" Even though I saw nothing and heard nothing else, I felt myself stiffen. Suddenly, there was a roar and some metallic clattering; and I "came back to life," so to speak, and saw nothing but road ahead.

I looked in the rearview mirror and saw the tail and clearance lights of the truck and the dark silhouette of the bridge receding behind me in the little bit of light left by the glow of the sunset. Having gotten a bit shaken up, I decided to stop when I got to higher ground away from the river, got out of the car, and watched the sky for any further activity, at least that's what I told myself I was doing. After having recovered somewhat I continued home. I have puzzled about this often and wondered who or what actually guided me through the bridge and who or what used the voice, which I have since heard in recordings, and I think it may have been my own voice that said, "Don't move."

Later in my life, I'm attending the University of North Dakota (UND), and having taken a bunch of exams and lost a lot of sleep studying, I'm driving home for a few days before I have to head back for more of the grind. I'm finally relaxing and have about forty miles more of the two-hundred-or-so-mile trip home when it got really quiet and things just sort of faded away. Suddenly, I'm awakened by mom's voice saying, Art-tea (Artie, the nickname which I had not heard said that way since I was fourteen) fairly loud.

Suddenly, I realized I'm accelerating past seventy miles per hour on the wrong side of the two-lane road and heading toward the left side ditch where there is an intersection to a farmer's field containing one of those corrugated steel culverts. Hitting that sucker would ensure the car would flip end over end and do nasty things to the driver. In those days, we didn't have seat belts or airbags either. It would not have been pretty!

You can bet I did some really fast maneuvering to get back to my side of the road and get the car back under control. Only in North

Dakota or maybe Wyoming can you hope to do something like this for any length of time without a head-on collision with another car. As soon as I could see a long way in both directions down the highway, I parked and got some fresh air. The rest of the trip was uneventful, and thinking about what had just happened kept me very wide awake!

Now that I reflect on it, I don't know why I studied so hard because no matter what I did, I pretty much had a predetermined grade on the first day of classes. We had three guys who dominated the grading curve: one with a photographic memory, one who could read something once and tell you everything it said in his own words, and one who did have to study some but remembered every equation and every fact after maybe reading it a few times.

We had seventy-five students who had declared their major as electrical engineering, and fifteen of us ended up with that degree. I know one who switched to medical school, and a bunch switched to math and other sciences. Just before graduation, our department head said they should not have graded on the curve. A little late, don't you think? Good thing about civil service, they give you their own exam, and it got me an offer at the next offered grade level (GS-7 instead of GS-5) for new employees in the engineering fields. Yep, the gross salary I made was about half as much per year as my total college debts!

My exciting driving trips continued after I had graduated college in August 1962 and had a job in California as an electronics engineer working for the Navy, testing aircraft and miscellaneous weapons. I packed my stuff into my mercury sedan (didn't have much to pack) and drove 2,100 miles or so to California, stopping along the way in Colorado, and visited two brothers in the Leadville area, which made the trip seem a little shorter; but it was still a long way for a farm kid.

The trip through Utah had some of the most amazing scenery I had ever seen; but on two-lane highways, it was slow going most of the time with all the trailers, trucks, and campers. Got to Las Vegas, which was tiny (about sixty-five thousand but still bigger than any city in North Dakota at the time) compared to what it is now. And it really slowed the trip because the main highway was the strip.

At that time, there was no speed limit in Nevada, so if traffic wasn't terrible, you could make up some of the time wasted going through Las Vegas. Las Vegas doubled in population in the next ten years. UND messed me up when I transferred from a quarter system community college to a semester system, and they insisted I didn't have enough math credits. So that's why I graduated in August instead of June, having had to make up the credits.

So with all the beautiful pictures of California, you don't expect that the lowest, hottest, most miserable deserts are in the state; and so it is a shock to encounter what I did. Just after sunset, I saw "Welcome to California" on the sign just before the sandstorm hit. All of a sudden, I'm in almost blackout conditions with sand blasting the side of the car, making it almost impossible to drive but afraid to stop because I could get hit from behind. Steering became a wrestling match and seeing was hit and miss, but once in a while, I could see the center line. Headlights ahead were very dim and so were the ones behind, but they actually helped me stay on the road.

In those days, this was also a two-lane highway. I survived that part of the trip and stayed the night in Barstow, thinking I was going to see lush grass and beautiful trees in the morning. News flash, all of Southern California is desert including the coast, and the only reason anything is green is because of irrigation or plants that survive by absorbing the little bit of moisture in the air or have roots so deep they get some groundwater. I had forgotten that we stayed overnight in Barstow when I went to San Francisco in 1955, so I should have remembered it was in the desert.

I continued my trip, in spite of wanting to turn right around and go home, through San Bernardino and into Los Angeles. By now, my windshield and right-side windows were hazy from being sandblasted the night before, but the full effect of the Los Angeles freeway system was still some experience. In spite of having lots of lanes, there are so many cars that all the lanes fill up beyond capacity so that every fifty feet or so, you come to a complete stop even in 1962; and all of them are spewing the most horrible exhaust, turning the air green or gray (not sure which) that burns your eyes, which adds to the haziness I am seeing.

Also, the freeways tend to subtract or add lanes at random, so you must stay very alert to where you are going. After surviving the trip though the downtown area of Los Angeles and into the San Fernando valley area but not being alert enough, suddenly, I found myself heading not west toward Oxnard but north toward Bakersfield. Grabbing the map, I discovered I could still go through Simi Valley on State Highway 118 and get to Oxnard that way.

I got on 118 and found out it was closed ahead due to a brush fire. I backtracked back down to US-101 and continued to my destination. I went into the first bar I found and ordered a beer, and after I drank it, I discovered that no one in the place except the bartender had been speaking English. He obviously was bilingual. Did I go too far south? No, this is Oxnard, California, all right. The sign said so.

I tried to make it home every year on vacation, and an unusual event happened on one of those trips. I was on my way to North Dakota in 1966. I had been battling wind and rain almost all day from Colorado through Nebraska and South Dakota into North Dakota on US-85 and finally had a respite from the rain as I approached US-10 (now I-94), which at that time was only two lanes. I turned east heading toward Bismarck about the time the nighttime speed limit would kick in at fifty-five miles per hour.

Heck, I hadn't been able to drive the daytime limit of sixty-five in North Dakota or seventy in South Dakota anyway because of the rain, which had finally let up. I had driven several miles when I realized I would be heading into more bad weather long before I would get close to Bismarck where I would again turn north toward Minot on US-83. The weather ahead looked absolutely horrible with continuous lightning flashes.

I found a road (ND-22, I think) that I knew would get me north and miss the weather, and I could cut across to US-83 north to Minot through Newtown on ND-23. Also, I didn't expect any Highway Patrol to be on that road, and I could make up some lost time, so I kicked it up to seventy miles per hour. I had gone a long way up that road when, suddenly, I had a panic attack. I had a sudden feeling of dread, but I convinced myself it was just nerves for about ten seconds and then the panic got much worse.

I felt like I may be having a heart attack or something; so I slammed on the brakes, put the car in neutral, set the hand brake, and got out to get some fresh air. I left the engine running and the headlights on high beam as I looked around to try to figure out what was wrong. I then felt okay, so I almost got back in the car to continue the trip. But suddenly, the panic was back and it felt worse than ever.

I started walking ahead to see if there was a horrible accident or something, maybe dead people or animals. I saw nothing in the headlights that would indicate a problem, and I was actually feeling relieved from the panic attack. But I thought I had better see if I could discover what was wrong anyway. I did hear water running ahead, and it sounded like a lot of it was moving by. But I still saw nothing.

It started to sprinkle a little rain, and suddenly, I saw what looked like little amber fireflies flashing momentarily in the air ahead. I puzzled over that for the next ten feet or so when I got to the source of the light and looked down to find a highway barricade with three flashing amber lights about five feet below the highway level where the riverbank had collapsed along with the highway. It had dropped straight down about eight feet and was still upright on part of the asphalt highway that had been undermined by the river.

Because I hadn't seen anything to give me a clue that anything was wrong, I puzzled over why I was still alive and not smashed in the car and drowned. Trying to rationalize my situation, I looked around to see if there were signs of any cars (lights or anything) that had gone off the cliff that I may have seen disappear from view suddenly or something. However, I don't think I could have done anything if that had happened. I hadn't learned to swim.

I finally accepted the fact that I had seen no disappearing cars or clues to the road being washed out at all and the miracle that I was still alive. After I composed myself a little, I went back to the car, turned around very carefully, and drove a short distance when I started getting extremely tired. I had a chocolate bar with crumbled peanuts in it, so I ate that but was soon extremely tired again. Totally exhausted after my long drive in the rain and what I may call a near-death experience, I pulled the car over to the side of the road, shut off the engine with the car in first gear, shut off the lights, set the hand brake, reclined my seat (it was a Rambler), and went to sleep.

I woke up fairly early as the sun came up and resumed the trip back to highway US-10. I reported the bridge and/or highway out to an attendant at the first gas station I came to and filled the tank so I wouldn't need to stop for gas later. Maybe twenty minutes or so later, I felt lousy like I had the flu coming on and soon was throwing up on the side of the road. My stomach area was burning up, mostly on the right side. I thought, *Oh God, are you going to let me die now after what I went through last night?* It finally went away but left a sore area on the right side of my abdomen. I didn't realize at the time, but I had just survived another attack of appendicitis. It must have been a piece of peanut lodging in the entry to my appendix that was the culprit this time. After I felt I could drive again, I finished the trip without incidence

Having had these three driving experiences, I concluded that something was very much interested in keeping me alive to accomplish something or maybe help bring other life-forms similar to myself into the world. I'm not sure when that something is going to give up and decide it's not worth keeping me around. At that time, I hope it just lets me go to sleep and not wake up and doesn't plan some painful or gruesome way to end it all like SEBS! SEBS is not styrene-ethylene-butylene-styrene in this case (see chapter 7). So far, it has had me live a very weird life filled with surprises, spirits, strange encounters, and stuff I will attempt to explain my theories on later in this book.

There was another fairly recent (maybe twenty years ago or so) happening that seems to fit the pattern of some sort of intervention that, after thinking about it, I thought was worthy of mention. I have been an amateur astronomer for most of my life and had built a 17.5-inch reflecting telescope that I took to star parties and was taking it to the Riverside Telescope Makers Conference (RTMC) at a scout camp near Big Bear Lake, California, where the night sky is pretty clear but still nothing like North Dakota skies.

I got off work and got ready to go and thought I would be there in time for the Friday evening meal that I had included in the weekend admission tickets I had bought. I checked the gas gauge and decided I could make it to Redlands, California, where I would get gas before I started the climb into the mountains to the campsite. Suddenly, I was bothered by the thought I should get gas in Ventura, California, which was already behind me about six miles into the trip.

The thought seemed to be dumb but very persistent; so I exited the freeway, got back on in the other direction, and backtracked to my favorite gas station, which was owned at the time by my son's first soccer coach. When he had coached the team, they won every regular season game that year. Doing this caused me to lose about thirty minutes and possibly be late for the evening meal at RTMC. The trip seemed to be going smoothly, and traffic was not as bad as typical Friday evening traffic normally was on I-10 east of Los Angeles.

Checking the time, I thought I may make the evening meal after all, but the thought was premature because suddenly, a Highway Patrol car passed everyone with lights flashing and began to weave back and forth on the freeway to stop traffic. After we all stopped, he got out of the patrol car and proceeded to put traffic cones across the freeway next to an exit, a very convenient one right there, and motioned everyone off the freeway. He had put one of the traffic cones right in front of my car; so I backed up slightly, opened my window so I could look out to see where the cones were, then started to go around the cone to the left.

The cop started yelling at me to go the other way and get off the freeway. As he put it, "There was a multicar accident up ahead with a lot of dead people." So I did the sensible thing to do and turned to the right, thus dragging one of the cones about ten feet before it exited from under my car. He got upset about that too, so I'm thinking, *Gee, I can't win!* I got off the freeway and did the opposite of what everyone else was doing and went left at the street we exited on and turned east on a street that paralleled the freeway on the north side that seemed to be a main street in the area.

I thought I may as well have dinner and maybe the freeway would be clear after dinner, so I stopped at the first family restaurant I found. I took my time with the steak I ordered, but even after I left the restaurant and when I could see the freeway, the traffic was not moving or was moving very slowly. I drove about twenty miles on the street, saw flashing lights where the accident must have been, and I could then see some movement on the freeway. So I went back on it as soon as I could find a cross street to get there.

Now I began to think about how my drive may have ended up had I not stopped for gas when I did. Somehow, I think I would have been in the middle of a bunch of smashed vehicles, possibly among the dead. To add more to the mystery, when I returned from the RTMC going through Redlands on Sunday, I noticed the gas station I had intended to use was surrounded by a fence and had machinery that was there to dig up and change the tanks so it must not have been open on that Friday anyway, but I hadn't noticed it that day because I had been on a one-way street going east and the gas station was on a one way going west. I guess it was a two-for-one psychic experience that may have saved my life again, and I got the gas I needed for the whole trip where I could get it most easily.

A recent walking event happened that may fit the pattern of preventing disaster also. Our kids and their families had helped me build most of our fence, but the back fence had not been replaced and was getting quite wobbly so it blew over in 2017 in a typical windstorm we have periodically. I had cleared away all the lumber from the fence and taken it to the dump, so the area was all clear to replace the fence.

I had a bunch of lumber drying on the front patio by the front fence gate and was planning on finishing the back fence over the last weekend in November 2017. Since I am now the chief cook and bottle washer in our household, I had cut up asparagus to have with our dinner. As usual, I decided to go outside and toss the inedible parts in what used to be our garden to add mulch because I thought it may become a garden again in the future. The last vegetable garden we had was pretty much destroyed by gophers, so I was thinking about later constructing planters inaccessible to critters.

Unfortunately, I flipped the wrong light switch as I went out the front door to take the stuff out there, said a four-letter word about the porch light being burned out (which it was not), and for some reason, the streetlamp across the street was not lighting up either so it was quite dark out. I approached the gate and suddenly found myself face down on the patio by the gate, and I was bleeding on my forehead and nose. I had forgotten the lumber was piled that close to the gate.

We called Phyllis, and she took me to the emergency room where I got four stitches on my nose and one on my forehead. Before I got the stitches, I had tried to reach forward to shake the doctor's hand and found I could not do so, and my shoulder hurt worse than I had ever felt before. She told me I had a bad sprain after she looked at the X-rays and didn't see anything broken and put my arm in a sling.

I didn't finish the fence as planned. I think my not finishing the fence may have saved our house on December 4, 2017, when the Thomas fire burned down six houses around ours and destroyed most of the fence we had built. Had I finished the fence, there would have been that much more wood at the top of our back hill to create more embers. We had a lot of exterior damage and windows to replace, but the house was intact and not much smoke got in.

The fire department couldn't do much because the fire had knocked out the waterline pumps, so the fire hydrants were empty. We still have our house, while they are building some of the homes around us. Some lots are not being worked on at all and are growing great crops of weeds. As I write this in early 2020, mine has a great crop of weeds too.

I didn't have a bad sprain as the emergency room doctor thought. I had completely destroyed my right rotator cuff, but that wouldn't show up in X-rays. Because of the smoke in the area, I didn't get an MRI on the date we scheduled. I didn't get the call from the facility to reschedule because they called my home phone where the line had been fried. I had to wait to get back on the schedule after I showed up for the appointment and found them closed.

I had surgery in August 2018, and I now have a complete reverse shoulder joint replacement, which is working great. The surgeon who performed the operation is amazing. With all the muscle damage I had, it is amazing how he got everything so that I can actually use the arm. Then, I got the best physical therapy possible and am really happy with the way the arm works now.

11

More Dreams, Intuition, and Weird Events

This chapter starts about two years after Gloria and I were married and before we had any children. We had used every weekend to explore as much of Southern California as we could. My job kept me very busy, and there was quite bit of overtime involved and not all weekends were available for fun exploring trips either.

Working for the Navy, I worked on some really interesting projects involving missile testing, one of which was one of the first smart bombs (SBs) called Walleye, a television-guided—once the pilot had locked on a target and released it—five-hundred-pound bomb. After release, the SB was totally on its own with no further inputs from the pilot.

It had a gyro-stabilized TV camera in the nose to guide it to the target at a point that the pilot had locked it onto. We had built an instrumentation pod that hung on the bomb-carrying aircraft to record the SB TV signal that the pilot saw before he locked on a target and launched the test weapon. It had a Sony videotape recorder which, in those days, was about one-third the size of a refrigerator that recorded the TV signal on a reel-to-reel two-inch-wide tape.

We had to glue parts in place on the circuit boards so it could withstand the airborne environment, using RTV, which was rubbery glue that would cure in a fairly large glob when exposed to the air. The pod was built out of a three-hundred-gallon external stores fuel pod that we modified. We had installed a special connector on it that would disconnect easily if the pilot had to jettison the pod in an emergency.

I know the connector worked well because a pilot had, by accident, launched one of our pods at China Lake, California. It fell away fine! We built several of those pods. The Walleye had a special connector too, but it was more complicated than the one on our pod. One night, I had a dream that something really terrible had happened at work and I was having a conversation with the program manager. The only part of the dream I remembered at all was his saying, "We've done so well so far. We better not drop the ball now!"

The next morning, I told Gloria about this *dumb dream* I had had and told her as far as I knew there were no problems at work. Not to worry! A few weeks later, the program manager called. It was on a Thursday. He said we had to get one of our instrumentation pods reconfigured to go on a fleet aircraft and get it ready to go to an aircraft carrier by Monday morning. It was to be used to record video data under actual combat conditions to help train other pilots on operating the SB.

Another of our recorders was to go with it for playback of the recordings. The catch was we couldn't change the aircraft in any way except to put a video isolation amplifier into the aircraft video-switching unit. We had to use the missile umbilical connector to get power and provide video into the pod. We would have to redesign the pod wiring to be compatible with the aircraft weapons control system and make it look like a smart bomb to the aircraft system, so redesign it I did.

The program office provided us a connector from a Walleye SB with the wires cut off, but it still had the connector pins in it, and the wires were too short to splice wires to them. Another problem was we didn't have the tool to remove the connector pins. We ordered one of them with an emergency requisition through our supply department, but the manufacturer said they wouldn't be making any of them for some time and they were completely out of stock.

We did have the pins to put in the connector if we could get the others out of the connector. I realized that the copper refills for government-issued ballpoint pens looked about the right size, and if we filed it with a jeweler's file so it had three prongs on the end, it may release the pins. What do you know, *it worked!* Only problem now was they broke after one or two uses. The connector had forty-one pins!

After filing and refiling several of these things, we were in business. By Sunday morning, I had redesigned the pod completely, and it was assembled and wired and we were checking it out when the special power converter that converted aircraft 3 phase 115 volt 400 cycle per second, now called Hertz (Hz), power to single phase 115 Volt 60 Hz used to power the videotape recorder failed. At the time we did this, cycles per second (cps) was in use, not Hertz.

We pulled one out of another pod, installed it, turned it on, and it failed the same way. I called the program office and told the program manager what had happened, and we discussed our options. Then he said, "We've done so well so far. We better not drop the ball now!" He called the CEO of the company that built the power converter, and the CEO and a technician were out that afternoon to repair our power converters. The company CEO told us that they had just discovered the problem with the converters a few weeks before and were getting ready to retrofit any unit that had failed, and ours were the first ones that had been sold to get the fix.

The pod left for Southeast Asia on Monday morning aboard the USS *Bon Homme Richard* (CV-31) aircraft carrier. When I told Gloria what happened, she told me I wasn't nuts and she remembered our talking about the dream. Maybe this explains why we think things that happen have happened before (déjà vu). When the pod was crated and shipped back to us after it had served the purpose, we found that all the big parts on the circuit boards were all leaning at an angle toward the forward end of the pod. This was because the last thing they had seen under flight conditions was the sudden stop as the plane landed on the aircraft carrier the last time.

The circuit boards were also full of fungus from the humid air on the carrier. Five years or so after this was all over, we received the connector pin removal tool through the Navy supply system after the connector company decided to build some. By then, the project was way in the past and it wouldn't have even made a good paperweight because it was too light.

About three years after we were married, Gloria and I brought our first child into the world, a little girl named Phyllis, who grew and developed rapidly, then a little over two years later we gave her a little brother we named Chad. She loved her little brother, and she also loved picture storybooks and never tired of having us read them to her. She would pull out the books she wanted read from the bookshelf, and after we read them, she would put them all back. She sometimes "read" the books to Chad, reciting from memory, I suspect. Soon, they were both into the books.

We often heard Phyllis talking in her room, sometimes when she was supposed to be going to sleep. We assumed she was talking to an imaginary friend like we all seem to at one time or another when we were kids. I listened quietly at her bedroom door to one of her conversations and realized she would talk a little while, then pause as though she was listening to someone, talk again, and so on. It sounded like a real conversation like she was talking on a phone or something, but it was too low for me to catch what she said. She did have a toy phone, so we thought maybe that is what she was playing with.

One day after we put the books away, the TV was on, and a rerun of the show *The Monkeys* was on. They were a musical group that had a comedy show and did some singing and playing along with some nutty antics. This particular one was about them in a haunted house, being chased by ghosts, running through doors in the hallway, in one door, out a different door, sometimes on the opposite side of the hall. You know the drill!

One of them ran into a bedroom and opened the closet door and beheld a glowing figure sitting in a rocking chair. All of a sudden, Phyllis got all excited and said, "There's Grandpa Seter!" I asked her where she had seen him and she said, "He talks to me in my room."

We had traveled to North Dakota when she was eight months old to go to his funeral, but I don't know if she saw him in the coffin. He had to have told her who he was, and the person in the rocking chair did resemble him somewhat. But it happened so fast I didn't get a real good look. Have you ever tried to get details on anything from a three-year-old? It drove me crazy because I knew what she told us was actually happening, and I wanted to know so much more.

Whenever I asked about what they talked about, she would change the subject. It was as though he had told her not to tell us anything because maybe we would think she was crazy if she did or something. I still want to know what they talked about. Literature I have read indicates that souls tend to reincarnate together life after life with relatives, with some exceptions, so I wonder now if Dad communicated or tried to communicate with all his grandchildren somehow. Or if not, why my daughter specifically? With that thought, I have speculated could Mom's soul incarnated be communicating with her former husband's discarnate soul? Wow, what a thought! If so, I don't ever want her to be hypnotized to remember her previous life because I really don't want to know exactly why she said, "Insanity reigns where you are!" Maybe I don't want her to remember either! But I would love to know what she and Dad talked about.

My sister Marcia had an interesting revelation from her daughter when her daughter was about the same age as Phyllis was when she talked to Dad. She had scolded her for something when her daughter said, "My other mother was nicer than you are." Marcia told me she had often talked about her "other mother."

Many of us human beings have had what many others have called imaginary friends, but I have come to the conclusion they may not be so imaginary after all. My younger sister had a friend with a very common name, Linda, and talked to her a lot. I had heard several of the conversations, and the one side I heard made a lot of sense and sounded more like someone talking on the telephone and that she was listening to a response to what she was saying.

One time, she was upset by something Linda had said. I was told I had a friend too, but the name convinces me that I couldn't have made it up because it was much more complicated. First, you need to understand that I was a shy kid; and at six years old on my first day of school—we didn't have kindergarten and preschool—when the teacher asked my name, I said my first, middle, and last name all together as a single name. Luckily, I had an older brother and sister attending the one-room school to tell her who I was and how my name was spelled.

My friends' name, when I was maybe three or four years old, was phonetically Ballaveenie, Balleveenie, or Balliveenie. I don't know which is closest to what I called him or her. How could a little kid come up with a name that sounded more like some alien being from another planet in some science fiction novel? At the time he or she was around, I could not pronounce certain letters, so maybe it was a first and last name put together as a single name.

Could that name have been Paul or Paula bunched together with some last name like Feeney? Could the last name have been something like Avery, Eveny, or a name starting with *V* or some other letter that I made to sound like *V*? I have puzzled about this and even asked Google for names starting with *V* and *F*, and there are millions of them, one of which was Veney and another was Vemuri. Whenever Dad talked Norwegian or even some English words, he would pronounce *W* like *V*, so maybe that puts another wrinkle in it.

No way could I figure out what that name was. I also wondered if maybe it was my mean little brother, and I was trying to say "Paul the weenie." I am quite sure my imaginary friend was a real person at one time and my soul was communicating with his soul and that he could have been either incarnate or discarnate at the time. That would be a blast if two souls communicated with each other that way for a while when both were occupying living bodies and could remember what was said. If that could happen, I wonder if it would be limited at all by distance. I don't think it would be limited at all.

We moved from a three-bedroom house in East Ventura to a four-bedroom two-story house next door to a similar family to our own with a boy and a girl close in age to our children. With four bedrooms, one of which became a sewing room/library, we had room to spread out and accumulate a lot more junk! We were very close to a park where the kids could play and have lots of room to run around, and life was good but not normal for long. Although the next chapter includes our children, the following events happened after they had left the nest and are somewhat spread out in time. They did not happen all at once.

One night, we heard someone walking back and forth from our bedroom down the hall to what used to be Chad's bedroom, and it went on as long as and as many times we were awake. Both Gloria and I heard it, and it was unmistakable because upstairs in the house, the floorboards under the carpet have always made noises as you walk on certain places. We didn't sleep much that night as we heard it all night long, and it was a bit scary.

I had gotten up when we first heard it to see what it was and saw absolutely nothing that could explain what we were hearing. A few days later, I was walking from our den into the kitchen when I felt a presence in the house and then felt a sudden feeling of confusion. I had a very sudden and alarming thought, *I'm dead!* I actually was so convinced I was dead that I looked back at the chair that I had been sitting in, didn't see myself sitting there, and so I went into the bathroom to inspect myself in the mirror.

Everything seemed normal, so I walked into where Gloria was sitting in the living room, and she acknowledged my presence. I knew then it wasn't me that was dead but some entity that may have passed right through my body. This is a really weird thing to have happen to you and is the sort of thing that really makes you question your sanity!

Gloria's dad was ill in the hospital in Colorado, and Gloria had wanted to go see him but couldn't because she herself had just had major surgery. She decided to sleep in what used to be Chad's room so I would not poke her incision or hurt her by moving around in the bed. One Saturday night, I felt a presence in our bedroom, and I thought it was Gloria needing something. However, when I looked, I saw no one. I still felt someone standing in the bedroom, and I also perceived some confusion on the part of whoever it was.

That someone then walked down the hall to Chad's old bedroom, the usual creaking floorboards when someone walks down the hall. I looked at the clock and saw it was about two thirty in the morning. Now I got to worrying that Gloria's dad had passed away, but I decided not to say anything to her until we got word from her mom or sister. Since no one called by late afternoon that day, I told Gloria what happened and that someone must have died but I didn't know who it was.

On Monday, Clair called and told us his mother-in-law had passed away sometime Saturday night between ten in the evening and six in the morning. I wonder what he thought when I told him it was at three thirty in the morning (Colorado time). Interesting that I heard the usual creaking floor as she walked down the hall because she had had both legs amputated because of diabetes.

Her family and Gloria's family had attended the same church in Colorado, the one we were married in, and were very good friends, so I guess she stopped by to say goodbye. They had visited us several years before, so she knew where we lived. But I doubt that even matters to a spirit. They seem to appear wherever they want to be at that moment. Obviously, she had her legs back or the floorboards wouldn't have made a sound.

I wonder though how a spirit could create enough pressure to make noise in the floor. Maybe I perceived somehow where she was and imagined the creaking floor, but then we both heard the noises created by the entity mentioned earlier so there must be actual pressure created on the floor. See, more questions with no real answers. I can go on and on that way!

We had been in Montana to attend sister Gretchen and Harold's fiftieth wedding anniversary and were about to go back through Colorado to stay with Gloria's parents for a few days before going home to California. I told Gloria I wanted to go to North Dakota to see our old neighbor Eddy before we went home, but her dad had been ill again so she wanted to get to Colorado fast. I relented even though I had a hunch that it was my last chance to see Eddy.

In spite of my urge to go to North Dakota, we continued the trip to Colorado as planned, and her dad seemed to have gotten a bit better but still not good. A few weeks after we got back to California, I called Marcia in North Dakota and asked, "How is everyone up there?" She said everyone was okay in the family but that our old neighbor Eddy had passed away the week before.

The following events happened after Phyllis was married and gave us two of our first four grandchildren. In 2003, Gloria and I toured the Reagan Library, which is in Ventura County, and I decided to buy a USS *Ronald Reagan* belt buckle. It was shortly before or after the ship was commissioned, I don't remember which. I was wearing it when we attended a special occasion at Phyllis's house. I was sitting on her couch waiting for the birthday person to get ready to open gifts. I thought to myself, *I should take this opportunity to show everybody the new belt buckle I bought for myself* when, all of a sudden, my granddaughter Mina, who was about two-and-a-half years old, looked at me, came over, and pointed to the belt buckle and said, "I bought that belt buckle for you!"

She said it like I may say it looking in a mirror. She kind of got a funny look on her face like she was thinking, *Why did I say that?* Phyllis says Mina was always saying things Phyllis is thinking about. Or Mina would be asking, "Are we going to [somewhere Phyllis is thinking of taking the kids but hasn't said anything about yet]?" How was she able to tune in to the thoughts of others when she was young? I will speculate on that later too.

You may wonder if I am a little bit psychic why I'm not wealthy having won a lot of money in Las Vegas or in the stock market. It doesn't seem to work that way at all. Only once was I "lucky" in Las Vegas, and I didn't even get to keep the winnings very long. We went to Las Vegas to meet my brother Gordon and sister-in-law Betty from Montana, where we stayed a couple days. Gloria and I went to see a show that night while they gambled at Keno and slot machines.

In the morning before we went to breakfast, we passed through the casino (you can't go in and out of the rooms without passing through some part of the casino), and a particular slot machine near the restaurant caught my eye. There was a lady at the machine at the time, and she did not seem ready to leave as she had just gotten more quarters to feed it. We had breakfast, then on the way out of the restaurant, I found she was still on that machine. So I looked around for another machine, but the one she was at was the only one that interested me, so I just waited and wandered around some more.

I played a bit of Keno and watched what other gamblers were doing while I waited. She finally left after losing some more money, and I took over the machine. I would almost use up the twenty dollars I had put in when the machine gave me back most of it or a little bit more. That continued to happen for almost two hours, and I was having fun so I kept at it. Suddenly, I won five hundred dollars, and just as suddenly, I lost interest in gambling at all so I quit.

I did have a couple of their silver dollars I got in change at the restaurant in my pocket, so when we were about to leave to go home, I put them in a dollar slot machine and got four dollars back. Then, we left to go home. As luck would have it, medical bills for Gloria came in the mail, and we owed a little over five hundred dollars.

Smoking and quitting

This may seem like a strange place to be talking about smoking, but it does kind of lead to some more weird events. It starts when I was a teenager and ends just a few years ago. I don't really remember exactly how old I was, but I was a teenager when I started smoking and this is how it happened.

Two of my older brothers who smoked and I, along with a friend of Eddy's, went to Eddy's house for a night of drinking a few beers and playing Canasta. Of course, I was an extra person and supposedly too young, so I did none of those things. But my job was to use a cigarette-rolling machine, a can of tobacco, and cigarette papers to create the cigarettes they smoked that night.

It took a little while to set up the machine each time. I was drinking Coke and had a few of them to stay awake. Soon, the room was filled with smoke, and my eyes were kind of burning from it and I was just barely keeping up to the job of supplying enough cigarettes. I was amazed at how fast they were being smoked. In the wee hours of the morning, they ran out of tobacco at about the same time they decided they had enough of the card games. We called it a night and went home.

For a few days after, I felt an urge for more of the smoke but didn't get it until I managed to steal one of my brother's cigarettes. It burned my throat and caused me some coughing, but I was now officially a smoker. I continued the lousy habit until I was thirty. I had a close call once when I had one hanging from my lips. I was carrying one of my nieces and she almost grabbed it, but I turned my head in time for her not to get burned.

That, as well as I was about to be a dad myself when my daughter Phyllis was about to be born and another fact, caused me to quit cold turkey. I had taken a carton of cigarettes, Pall Mall, the long unfiltered ones to work on Monday morning and found I was taking the last pack out of it on Wednesday evening. That meant that either someone else was using my cigarettes or I was smoking more than three packs a day, and I'm pretty sure it was the latter.

Thinking, *I've got to quit,* I wrapped three layers of scotch tape completely around all sides of the pack and put it in my shirt pocket. The way it worked is I kept telling myself I would have one at some future time about an hour or so away. I was very busy most of the time; so often, the time passed and I would tell myself, *Shucks, I missed it. Now I have to wait another hour or so.* If the time I had set to take a cigarette arrived and I noticed it, I would convince myself I could wait another hour.

Two weeks later, the scotch tape was a bit tattered but still covered the whole pack. I had unconsciously tried to remove it, but it was still pretty much intact. I kept the pack in a dresser drawer for several months before throwing it away. Whenever someone lights up a cigarette and I can smell it, it still smells so good to me for maybe two to three seconds, but then it smells bad again. On trips across country after that, I could tell if someone in a car ahead of me was smoking; and when we went to Las Vegas, when smoking was allowed in the casinos, I would smell smoke for days afterward probably because it was embedded in my sinus cavities.

Andy had gotten married, divorced, and married again and moved his new family to the Seattle area where he worked with his brother for a while, then started his own business. We kept in touch by phone periodically, and he would usually call when his wife was on a trip somewhere for her business. We noticed he seemed to be a bit inebriated sometimes when he called, and he seemed to be more so as time went by.

He was also starting to cough a lot; and one time, when I asked about his cough, he said that was my fault because I had started him smoking, which was a surprise to me. He developed heart disease, and his coughing and pauses to get his breath as well as slurring speech made it harder to understand him so it was quite apparent he was very ill. Sometimes, we thought it sounded like he paused to light a cigarette.

Some weeks after he passed away, another weird thing started to happen. Gloria was in the living room watching one of her shows and I was in the den watching one of mine when, suddenly, I smelled tobacco smoke which became quite strong and actually started to burn my eyes a little. Thinking one of our neighbors was smoking, I asked Gloria if she smelled it and she said she didn't. I went outside, and the air seemed to be fresh with no smell.

I walked around the house and looked around to see if anyone was outside smoking. I went back in the house and still no smoke smell for about two minutes. Suddenly, it was there again. This happened off and on for several months. When Gloria and I were together in the living room watching one of our shows together, we would both smell it. Later on, she would smell smoke when I didn't. I have no other explanation for this except that maybe Andy was visiting us.

Mina the medium

As I mentioned before, our granddaughter Mina has been very psychic, but an event happened that I cannot and actually don't want to forget because it verifies some of what I have concluded about a part of us living somehow after death.

First, a little background information is required to set the scene so to speak. When Mina was in middle school, she suddenly had spells that caused her to become paralyzed and collapse on the floor. She could sometimes pull herself up and slide on the floor using her hands. She would eventually regain her muscle control after minutes or what seemed like hours. It was a very scary time for all of us, and I can't imagine what she herself was feeling as she was experiencing this.

Many times, I had picked her up from school when Phyllis couldn't because she was taking one of her other children to doctor or dentist appointments or whatever. It took many months, seemed like years, that finally, doctors diagnosed that she had had West Nile Virus. She has had a bad struggle with side effects of that nasty little virus, but it didn't seem to stop her from having some interesting psychic events.

My brother Gordon passed away in July 2014. A few days after that, I spent part of the morning shopping for various things. I stopped to get money at the Credit Union ATM, got some plumbing material at Green Thumb, picked up beer and chamomile tea at Trader Joes, got mouthwash at CVS Pharmacy, and went to Vons to shop for groceries. When I went to checkout and was putting items on the checkout counter, I felt a presence behind me that seemed to be very close to me. I turned to see who it was and saw no one there, but the feeling that there was someone there was still very strong.

Later that morning, Phyllis called to ask if I could pick up Mina at the psychologist's office in the afternoon because she or Dan, our son-in-law, would not be able to. At that time, I do not think Mina had been diagnosed yet, and all kinds of specialists were still puzzling over her ailment. Even since the diagnosis, they have still been puzzling over how to make her life better but so far have not solved that problem at all and she still has episodes and other medical problems.

I went to pick her up and take her home, and when we were on the way, she suddenly seemed to stiffen, which scared me a bit because I thought she was having another episode. But she was listening to something. She would listen and then talk a short sentence, and it went like this.

"Grandpa, you had a brother that passed?"

I said, "Yes, Gordon. But I don't think you ever met him."

"He was at your house today."

Pause.

"You weren't home."

Pause.

"He saw Gloria and sat on the couch with her."

Pause.

"He looked for you."

Pause.

"He found you at the grocery store."

Pause.

"You were in the checkout area."

Pause.

"It was at Vons."

When I asked her and Phyllis if I could include this in the book, they said I could. "Go for it" and "okay" in that order. Mina doesn't remember doing this at all, but I suspect all the traumatic experiences she has had make this seem trivial. But I was pretty darned impressed she could get that much information from a spirit and pass it on to me.

What made it really believable was her use of the name Gloria because she always calls her grandma, and I don't think she has ever called her Gloria before this event or after. After thinking about it, she may have met Gordon once but wouldn't remember it because she was very young when we went to an anniversary event where he would have attended the event too. He must have still been with me when I went to get her. I wonder how he knew he could communicate through her. More questions I have. I may even have an answer, but that will be included in a later chapter.

12

Visible Spirits and Weird Things

My first experience with seeing a strange phenomenon was when I was about seventeen and Myron Shelton, a neighbor, and I had driven to where we could watch the sunset which looked like it was going to be something special; and we weren't disappointed.

We had driven to a spot where we could see the entire western sky with no obstacles in the way and observed one of the most spectacular sunsets I have ever seen. The oranges and reds were so vivid, and the rays of colorful sunlight were amazing. Too bad I didn't have a camera at the time. But the sunset is not what I am writing this about.

We sat and talked for a long time. He was eighteen and was going into the Army, so we were talking about all the fun times we had had and also had a little dandelion wine. I think he was a little concerned about going in the service and needed someone to talk to. We talked for quite a long time until it got dark and stars came out, and once again, the sky was looking really spectacular because the clouds had dissipated.

Then I saw it. Myron had a faint glow around him that surrounded his body. In places, it actually seemed to extend what I would guess about three-quarters of an inch in places from his body and face. At first, it startled me, and I was a bit scared. I looked at my hands to see if I could see anything like it on myself, and there didn't seem to be anything at all. In fact, it was dark enough that I could barely see them. I could see him almost clearly through the glow. After some time, it seemed to fade out to nothing. No, I was not drunk. Years later, I read about auras. That was the only time I ever saw one though.

When our kids were young, we kept our bedroom doors open so we would hear them if they had nightmares or needed a drink of water or milk or whatever. From our bed, we could look out into the hall. Where Chad's bed was in his room, he could see into the hall also. One night, I had had flu or symptoms similar to flu and had to be ready to race to the bathroom at a moment's notice, and had several times.

That night was miserably hot because of the east winds that blew in from the desert. In an effort to stay cool, we had a large square fan set up in the hallway to blow air into the three bedrooms. The light from the streetlamp shining through the window made everything in the hall quite visible. I had another bathroom call, so I got up and saw what I thought was Chad standing in the hall in front of the fan with his clothes rippling in the breeze of the fan but didn't say anything because I was kind of preoccupied.

I was sitting on the throne, and I thought, *Hey, what the heck was he wearing? That isn't how he was dressed when he went to bed.* All of a sudden, I heard Chad scream and come running down the hall and say to Gloria, "I saw a boy in the hall, but when I was looking at him, he disappeared." I sat there with the hair standing up on the back of my neck, thinking how are we going to sound convincing when we tell him it was just a dream. Phyllis later told us she had seen the boy sometimes and one time accompanied by a cat. She says she had seen just the cat in the backyard sometimes.

Gloria was feeling awful with a migraine, so I had done the clothes wash and was making Chad's bed when I suddenly saw a weird sight for maybe half a second. In the air above his bed, I thought I saw a black mouth with the tongue sticking out, giving me the raspberry. There was no sound with it. I was thinking, *Seter, you are losing it. That didn't happen.*

I finished the job, thinking I may be going nuts for sure, and then examining the area where I thought I had seen it, I saw nothing more. Later, I heard Chad telling Phyllis that he had seen it, and she pretty much laughed at him, saying it was all in his head. I decided not to say anything because I thought it would just freak him out more if he thought it was real and someone else had seen it too. I didn't want him to be afraid to be in his own bedroom. There were weird sightings of other stuff too, like a cat puppet that appeared in midair or, Chad said, at the foot of his bed one time; but I never saw any of those.

Things also happened at work. One morning at about four, I arrived at work to set up our telemetry (TM) station to support some early development Tomahawk Cruise missile tests that were to take place at five. The missile, hung on an A-6 aircraft we had installed support equipment in, in the hanger next door, required several hours to align its inertial navigation system (INS) before the A-6 could take off to fly to White Sands Missile Range to launch the missile there.

The long flight would simulate an actual cruise missile long-range flight and verify the navigation system. We had installed a display in the A-6 cockpit that indicated where the missile was attempting to fly. The pilot would have to fly by flight rules over major populated areas, so the missile computer would be constantly correcting its flight path and that would add useful flight test data. Wherever possible, the pilot "flew the needles" on the display controlled by the missile.

Before the test flight, we were to record the telemetry signal from the missile so that, in case something failed during the alignment process, the data could be analyzed later. Our building was configured with aircraft hangar space in the center and two-story sections on each end containing lab and office space. We had a machine shop in the hanger, laboratory spaces downstairs, and office spaces upstairs. I always entered the building on the east side because my office was upstairs on that end, and my key only opened that one door of the four entrances to the building.

There was what we called a "lab office" along with an equipment cage for checking out equipment to use in the shops in the north part of the hangar. Our TM station was on the west end downstairs, so after dropping off my briefcase in my office, I went downstairs across the south side of the hangar to set it up. I looked across the machine shop area at the lab office as I went by because the lights were on and I saw Bob (one of two shop foremen) standing by his desk, and I thought, *Gee. Why is he here this early?*

I had just passed out of sight of the lab office when it dawned on me that he had died of cancer a few weeks before. With the hair standing up on the back of my head (literally), I ran back to where I could see the lab office to find it completely dark with no one around at all. That's one heck of a way to start the day. I went into the almost totally dark room where the circuit breakers were, fumbled around to find the breaker panel, and turned all the breakers on to make sure that there were no dark spots anywhere in the hangar area.

I needed as much light about then that I could get, and shaking in my boots, I set up the TM station and called the contractors that were preparing the missile for launch to let them know I was ready. I had loaded two tape recorders with tape and started one of them when I saw the missile TM signal was being received in our telemetry receivers. The rest of the day went as I expected with no surprises, except I kind of doubted my sanity for the rest of the day.

The flight happened as scheduled, but the White Sands Missile Range became unavailable for safety reasons so the launch was scrubbed that day. I had to repeat the setup and recording three more times that week before we successfully had it launched. I had the willies every time I had to cross the hangar area but didn't see anything unusual during the three other mornings. I must add that the previous situation could not happen these days but only because labor unions would have been up in arms. I, as an engineer, would not be allowed to set up and operate the TM station. It would have to be done by technicians and shop helpers, I think.

During my career, I suffered through a management job for five years. I got to know Don, one of the other branch heads, as we were called, fairly well. We would go to the cafeteria in the mornings to discuss all kinds of stuff, some of it having to do with our jobs, over coffee. I had even confided in him that I was not attending church because of events that had happened all my life that caused me to doubt the church's teachings.

I said I didn't think there was a hell or that anyone understood who Jesus was and that he was more of an example for us and wanted to inform us about what was what rather than a savior. I said that I thought Jesus was totally misinterpreted about things he said. Don gave me an audiotape of a sermon that his minister in the Church of Religious Science had given. Basically, the minister said almost my exact words about Jesus. So off to the Church of Religious Science Gloria and I went for several years until that pastor retired and we weren't thrilled with the new one. We had gone on a trip to visit relatives, and when we came back, we just never went to the church again. But that was much later than the following events.

One day, I went to Don's office in another building to talk about a project we were working on. His office door was open, and I saw a very pretty woman standing there and he was talking. So I waited and talked to his resource assistant (secretary), Jeanine. I couldn't tell what Don was saying, but the conversation went on for quite a long time. I could see the lady in his office but not him because his desk was around the corner from the open door. She didn't appear to speak at all during the time I saw her, and I had watched her several times.

I wondered why Don had not had her sit in the chair that she was standing beside. The phone rang, and Jeanine answered it and told whoever was calling she would give Don the message. As she hung up, I noticed a light was still lit on the phone, which indicated that someone in the building was using that line, but eventually, it also went out. When Jeanine saw the light on the phone was off and I was still standing there waiting, she said, "Don is in there if you want to see him."

I started to say "But he has a visitor." Then I turned and looked in his office and could see no one standing there. If the person had left his office, she would have had to pass in front of me. No one did. I realized then I had seen the spirit of his daughter, who had been killed in a car accident. Several times when we went for coffee after that, I felt there were three of us there.

In fact, since we were both so open with each other about our beliefs, I told him about what I had seen at his office and the feeling I had about being accompanied when we were having coffee. He actually thanked me for sharing that because he had the feeling she was there too and I had just verified his feelings were correct. I actually surprised myself on how quickly I had confided in him and how he accepted the fact I saw his daughter's spirit.

Another day as I got off work, I called Gloria to see if she needed me to do any shopping on my way home and told her I was going to check on some movies and get paint for one of our rooms at home. I stopped at Video Time, which used to be at the corner of Main Street and Borchard Drive, and got a videotape to watch; and then I proceeded to the paint store. I was on Borchard Drive going south and stopped for a red light at Thompson Boulevard where there was an older man and woman (maybe in their seventies) with a younger lady (in her forties, I would guess) waiting to cross south across Thompson Boulevard.

At that time, the DOT was testing several types of road-marking material, so on the edge of the crosswalks, there was some type of really thick rubbery material. Thompson Boulevard seemed to be clear of traffic for a moment, so I started to make a right turn on red. Out of the corner of my eye, I saw a car coming West on Thompson Boulevard at what I estimated was somewhere around fifty to sixty mph. I slammed on the brakes and made an awful screech on that rubber strip with the front tires.

I looked at the three people waiting to cross and noticed the man staring at me with what looked like extreme anger. I'm thinking, *Geez, mister, I couldn't help that. What are you so angry about?* We were staring at each other for a couple of seconds when the light changed to green for me. I looked to the left to make sure all traffic had stopped from that way and was going to proceed after the three of them crossed the street.

The two ladies crossed the street. Where did the man go? He was nowhere to be seen, or at least if he was still there, I could no longer see him. I looked all around and did not see him. Did he go in the little restaurant on the corner? If he did, he's the fastest old man I ever saw. I noticed the building was closed, boarded up, and there is a for lease sign on it. I realized then I had just seen another discarnate spirit; and he had looked so real, so solid, and so angry. I proceeded to make the right turn to go get paint.

Then, something occurred that I know the exact date when it happened. At about one thirty in the afternoon on a Sunday, August 26, 2012, I was buying a ticket to see *2016: Obama's America* at the Century 10 Downtown Theater in Ventura, California. A couple about my age or maybe a bit younger accompanied by a young man, maybe teen or in his early twenties, walked up behind me.

I glanced back at them and grinned, thinking, *Someone else wants to see this movie!* I think it was the woman who said, "Jack"—I don't remember what name she said so I will call him that—"would have loved this."

As I walked away toward the door of the theater with ticket in hand, I heard the gentleman say, "Two adults please." I looked back to find only the couple at the ticket booth, no young man. Where had he gone? How fast can someone move? I don't know if it was significant or not, but I thought I had heard the sound of someone starting a motorcycle just before they bought their tickets, but that sound was only momentary so he couldn't have driven away on a motorcycle. Had I thought about it at the time, I would have gone back and asked the lady in the ticket booth how many people were behind me when I bought my ticket, but she probably would have thought I was nuts.

Before these events happened, I didn't think much about the people I passed on the streets or at street corners unless they were very attractive young ladies or I knew them. It never occurred to me that the fact there were either fewer or more people crossing the street than had been waiting at the corner to cross that some may not be flesh and blood. I thought they had either crossed the other way or changed their minds and had gone into stores or come out of stores to join the group crossing. Now I wonder if some were spirits, ghosts, or whatever because I can't be sure I haven't seen more of them. The only reason I knew the ones that I have written about were not like us is that they disappeared or I just could not see them anymore if they were still there. I don't know anyone living who can just disappear like that.

In hindsight, I realized that of the four spirits I saw, I knew that two of them were actually dead in this universe, and that will make more sense after you read later chapters. Not knowing the circumstances of the event at the corner of Borchard and Thompson, which is within blocks of a hospital, I have a question to speculate on. Were the two ladies going shopping at Pic 'n' Save to fill in time while the man was undergoing a surgical procedure and during the time he would be in recovery? Did he have a medical emergency and an out-of-body experience wherein he was accompanying the ladies on the shopping expedition when I saw him and was resuscitated and disappeared when he returned to his body?

Was the young man I saw at the theater actually dead in this universe; or was he in the military, in bed, sleeping and dreaming he was with his parents attending the movie, his soul actually accompanying them? Did he disappear only because I heard them asking for only two tickets; and my mind, realizing he wasn't there in the flesh, blocked me from seeing him? I believe our souls do a lot of things when we are sleeping and, in fact, when we are awake that we are not aware of. When we wake up, unless we were having what could be called a nightmare, it may seem strange that we forget our dreams so fast.

I was not a witness to this; but an incident occurred at Marcia's house in North Dakota the day her mother-in-law, Ellenore, passed away. Ellenore's husband had passed away some time before, and Ellenore lived with them for some time. Margaret, Tom, and their son Mike were visiting along with several other family members. No one remembers the reason for all of them to be there. Because bedroom space was all taken, Margaret was going to sleep in the living room with several children who were sleeping on the floor but was still up.

A short time after Ellenore's death, Mike, in his sleep, said in an old man's voice with a heavy brogue, "Ellenore, we have to go now." At the same time, Margaret saw Ellenore walking through the room stopping by each child, saying goodbye to them. One thing about this is she did *see* Ellenore but did not see Ellenore's husband even though she *heard* "his voice" spoken by her son.

Gloria says she sees one of the cats, now dead, we had around the house every once in a while. I have seen something resembling a cat out of the corner of my eyes, but nothing is there when I turn to look directly at the spot where I thought I saw it.

13

Ghosts and Hauntings Class

Since I have had so many experiences with spirits and strange events, I decided to attend a class presented by the Ventura County ghost hunter, Richard Senate. He told us that the reason we were attending his class was that we were all psychic because to see or perceive spirits we had to be "aware" in special ways that only psychics are.

He then proceeded to tell us about all the haunted places in the county and to tell us about the field trips we would make. During one of our sessions, he talked about a thing that happens to some people. He told us, "You have been home alone for some time, and you hear the other family members come into the house and all the sounds associated with their arrival (maybe even the sounds of the car coming, car doors closing and footsteps), but when you go to greet them, there is no one there. Maybe fifteen or twenty minutes later, the event repeats itself. Only this time, for real."

I was about to say, "Wow, you just described my life!" But he said, "This only happens to Norwegians!" I was speechless after that, thinking about what he had just said, so I said nothing. But I guess I wasn't nuts after all. But incidents like that happens to my daughter and grandchildren, so just a little bit of the Norwegian when mixed with other nationalities must be enough.

We went on several field trips, but one was very memorable. Gloria, Phyllis, and Chad went along on this one; and we went to a place called Olivas Adobe. The place was supposed to be haunted by a woman in a long dark-colored dress. While we were there, I kept seeing movements out of the corner of my eye, always gone when you look straight at the places.

Your eye is more sensitive to movement off center when the lighting is low. Phyllis said she looked at a picture in one room and actually felt like the presence was welcoming her. Richard Senate told her that many people had the feeling of welcoming, and some even felt like they were being embraced. He then had us "dousing for bodies."

Some people had been buried in the courtyard years ago, and he said as psychics, we should be able to find them. He lined up part of the group and handed us each two pieces of coat hanger bent into *L* shapes. He showed us how to hold them out in front of us and explained how they worked. Then, he told us to find the bodies.

My wires immediately started to move, so I followed to where they pointed. And as I walked, they moved inward and crossed over one point on the ground. I backed up, and they started to point forward again. I moved forward, and they crossed again. I looked around to see where I was to try to triangulate my position for future reference. I found a little sprig of grass that looked discolored by my left foot and thought that will be easy to spot.

I wanted to see if someone else would find exactly the same spot. I was a skeptic on this one even though I had felt the strange movement of the rods as though they had a mind of their own. I guess I doubted that I should have an ability to do it. Well, the person who took my place did find exactly the same spot. We weren't done though.

He had us group together the same way again and said, "Now we are going to find the head end of the bodies." The spot I found was about two feet farther than I had gone before and slightly to one side. The next person found exactly the same spot. I am now a believer! Phyllis found a body too. Water witches must be for real.

Apparently, there is a little something inside you that knows this information, and it comes out by your using little devices like bent wires. And of course, those Ouija boards that some people think are the work of the devil. "It is your subconscious making little micromovements in your muscles that you can't even feel," Richard Senate told us. It feels very strange how the wires seemed to just come alive and feel like they are moving on their own.

On another field trip, only those in the class took a bus to a hotel in Santa Paula called the Old Glen Tavern Inn. Supposedly, the lobby and rooms 218 and 307 are haunted. We went into one room (neither of those) where someone had found a real cold spot along one wall. I went over to see how it felt, and I found it to be extremely cold. I could really feel it on the back of my hand when I put it in one place.

I thought it was a cold draft, so I turned my hand over. Still cold on the back of my hand! We were in another room (don't remember which) when all of a sudden, the bed seemed to get an indentation like someone was sitting on it, or maybe we just imagined it did. I got the feeling that someone we couldn't see was in the room and that someone was really amused with all the company. I will say that the place had an interesting feel about it, but we didn't *see* any ghostly apparitions or shadows in any of the rooms. I did feel like we were being followed several times though when we moved from room to room.

Richard Senate has written several books on the subject and described many haunted locations he and his wife have investigated and/or written about other's accounts. They are very interesting.

14

Traveling

We traveled a lot as a family, and with Gloria's family and my big family spread out across the country, we had reasons to visit a lot of states. We have been in every state west of the Mississippi River, traveling by car as well as New York by air. We have been to many national parks in the western states.

When Phyllis was eleven and Chad was nine, we packed our car with food and water and made a short trip to Edwards Air Force Base to watch the landing of the Space Transportation System (STS) space shuttle *Columbia* return from the fourth STS mission on July 4, 1982. We passed hundreds of cars, campers, pickups, and even a few buses until we found a nice spot close to some portable toilets to park.

We ate some snacks as we waited for the event. After a while of waiting not too long, we heard the double sonic boom which announced that the shuttle would arrive very soon. We watched proudly as the shuttle made the turn for the final approach to then land flawlessly. There must have been thousands of pictures taken that day, and I used up most of my film.

We were really surprised when we got the extra bonus of watching a second STS vehicle, the space shuttle *Challenger* mounted on top of the Boeing 747, take off from Edwards AFB and make a couple of passes over the thousands of people before it headed out across country to deliver it to Cape Canaveral, Florida. It was a beautiful day out on the desert, and the whole event was thrilling. The only bummer about the whole thing is that the two vehicles we saw that day were the two whose flights would both end up in tragic accidents that would delay the STS flight program twice but worst of all the tragic loss of fourteen astronauts, including a schoolteacher.

Alaska

I had retired and had hoped we would travel some while we still could. Gloria's health was not good, and we never knew how she was going to feel from day to day and often had to cancel events we had planned to attend or travel to. Many days of her life were spent in bed with migraine headaches, arthritis, or other illness.

For several years, she was medicated with Fentanyl patches that would have knocked out a horse, but it only controlled her pain so it was bearable. But that was later in her life than what I am describing now. But I digress. We had planned a two-week cruise and land tour to Alaska and could hardly wait for the day when we would be on our way. We would fly from LAX to Vancouver, British Columbia, to board the ship and travel to various ports in Alaska, including Glacier Bay and a land excursion by bus and train to Carcross, Yukon Territory, then a land tour by bus and train in Alaska. It was going to be a fun trip.

About two weeks before the departure date, my attitude about our upcoming trip took a surprising reversal. Suddenly, I wasn't looking forward to the trip and I didn't know why. It was a total mystery why I had my doubts about the trip, but I couldn't shake the feeling it was not going to go as planned. It wasn't that Gloria's health had changed for the worse or anything like that, and in fact, she was doing quite well. She was still looking forward to the trip until my negativity rubbed off on her too. I had thought at first that maybe my doubts had been about her health, but I knew it was not so and that something else was wrong. We were reluctant to even pack our bags.

Finally, we decided we were going to get ready for the trip and packed, saying to ourselves and each other we were going to have a good time no matter what. We were trying to be positive even though we still had doubts, which were totally unexplainable. We were to meet the bus provided by the agency that arranged the trip. Chad took us to the meeting place and waited until we boarded the bus and left with the group to head for the airport.

We were almost to the airport when we saw the advisory sign on the freeway that said LAX IS CLOSED, to which the bus driver said, "That has got to be a prank. LAX never closes." We got to the airport to find it deserted except for security personnel who wouldn't tell us what was going on. They let us use the bathrooms in terminal 1 before we boarded the bus to go back home. That day, September 11, 2001, LAX was indeed closed. Someone on the bus called a friend who told her what had happened. We really didn't know the extent of the chaos until we saw it on TV later.

When I heard what had happened, I remembered a dream I had about two months before in which I was in ground school preparing to learn to fly an airplane. I had actually attended ground school several years before this but didn't finish because of my hectic job schedule and Gloria's health problems. In the dream, one of the students said he didn't care to learn to land an airplane, only to fly straight and level.

In the dream, I was shocked and thought this was totally insane and said that the first thing I want to learn is how to land a plane. If I'm up in the air in a plane, I want to return to earth the right way. Some months later, I heard on the news that one of the hijackers that took over the airliners when he was in flight school had stated he only wanted to learn to fly straight and level. Shouldn't that have been a red flag to someone that something about him was not right?

Princess Cruises sent us vouchers that we could use for a future trip, which we used in September 2002, and we had a great time. This time, we were excited about the trip and couldn't wait to get all packed and ready to go. We did all the extra excursions we could do in what seemed like such a short time. We never doubted that this time, the trip was going to be great, and it was.

Hawaii

Gloria and I also took a two-week cruise to four of the Hawaiian Islands on one of the ships that usually traveled to Alaska in the summer months. To our surprise, we had one of the same entertainers that performed on the Alaska trip. It was a fantastic trip with lots to see and great food. It was amazing to watch flying fish fly out of the water, and where they hit the water to see a bunch of other fish fly out of the water. That must have spread over the entire Pacific Ocean. Well maybe not that far!

We had a great time in the Hawaiian Islands and then watched the flying fish again. We had returned and were quite tired from the trip. We both slept well that night but were awakened early by the phone ringing. It was Phyllis asking us to come to her house to stay with Dominick and Mina, our grandchildren, while she went to the hospital to present us with another one.

My first sleepy thought was *How are we going to do that since we are on a ship?* But I soon realized that we were in fact in our beds at home. How fuzzy our brains get when we are tired from a great trip. We had fun over at her house with the grandkids watching movies, and Phyllis brought our grandson Christian into the world.

15

Spirit Intrusion in the Bedroom

As you may have noticed from what I have written so far, my life was quite normal and even what you could call boring or *humdrum*! Then on December 30, 2013, it got weird.

I have to go back several years before Gloria and I decided to sleep in separate rooms, so we could actually get some sleep, to provide some background. We were sleeping one night when I woke up to find a stone-cold arm between Gloria and me. I panicked, thinking Gloria had died during the night and she was already cold. Oops, that was my arm. Somehow, I had cut off circulation in my left arm and it was cold. I couldn't feel anything, nor could I move that arm. I got up and started massaging the arm and slowly got back feeling in it and soon was able to move it. I have to admit I was panicked for some time, thinking I may lose the arm. All was okay until the date mentioned above.

Sleeping alone and lying on my right side, the arm thing happened again, only this time it was the arm I was sleeping on, the right one. Upon half waking up with the feeling something was not quite right, I must have literally spun my body over to my left side, only as I turned, I felt pressure on that side and heard the sound of a woman laughing (at least it sounded like a woman's laugh). Now I am fully awake, and I literally jumped out of bed and turned on the light in the bathroom as it was the closest light switch.

I was alone in the room as far as I could tell, and the door was still closed as I had left it when I went to bed. I turned on more lights and checked everywhere in the room in the closet and under both sides of the bed. I went to Gloria's room, and she was okay and fast asleep so she hadn't been in the room. In fact, she was snoring louder than I had ever heard her snore before, but I could tell she was asleep for sure and not faking it.

After I got my arm working okay again, I spent quite a bit of the night actually trying to make the sound I heard by bouncing around, moving side to side and up and down on the bed, rolling quickly and everything else I could think of but gave up, never being able to duplicate it. Finally, I went back to bed, and eventually, I actually got some sleep. As the following events happened, I really wondered if I was hallucinating or even dreaming them because they seemed impossible.

The next night shortly after I got into bed, I got a ringing in my ears, a feeling like the pressure changed in the room, and heard a snapping sound in the room. My room being on the west side of the house is always warmer than other rooms, so I had on light covers. Suddenly, the covers seemed to get heavier on my legs, and the heaviness moved up over my waist unto my chest. I usually sleep on my side, but this started so quickly after I was in bed that I hadn't gotten to my sleeping position yet and was on my back.

The heaviness was accompanied by what felt like static electricity over my entire body. I felt anxiety, a bit of fear and anticipation. Why anticipation? Was I anticipating something or was someone else? My next reaction was to get out of bed, worried that I may be having a stroke like my dad had in his late sixties. I checked myself out to make sure there wasn't any numbness anywhere; everything that should move was actually movable and that my face seemed normal while I made faces at myself in the mirror in the bathroom.

I thought maybe static electricity was causing the covers to feel heavier but rejected that idea because that would not have explained why the little extra weight seemed to move around. After I went back to bed, everything seemed normal. Nothing out of the ordinary was happening, and after a while, I slept somewhat okay the rest of the night.

For many nights, but not every night, I had similar things happening except that a little fear went away after about three or four events and was replaced by curiosity on my part. I never saw anything that could account for what was happening, and it seemed to vary in intensity. Some variations occurred, such as sometimes feeling a brief pinching feeling on my cheek; pressure on my mouth; a few times something touched and moved my hair and sometimes accompanied by a slight odor: musty, gun smoke, hot metal, cigarette smoke, and spice of some kind to name a few.

Many times, I felt a presence in the room just before the events happened. It happened for a few months, and I told nobody about it because I didn't want anyone else freaking out about it. Sometimes, I was actually falling asleep during the events, so I didn't know how long they occurred each time. I usually wasn't moving while I was awake, and these things happened unless I was in an uncomfortable position. And when I did move, sometimes it stopped. I still wondered about static electricity maybe causing it, but it didn't happen only when the air was dry.

My curiosity was getting to the point where I had to see if I could see anything in the room as it happened. On January 19, 2014, I set up my Hi-8 tape camcorder on night shot to see if anything would show up; and that night, the event was very intense and lasted a long time. In the morning, I checked the camcorder to find that the tape had jammed and I had nothing. I had quite a time getting the tape out of the camera because it had pulled out far enough to engage the mechanism of the camera but didn't get pulled back into the cartridge when the camera shut off, probably after a few seconds when the camera detected the bad tape. That was the first and only time it had failed, and it turned out the cartridge was all messed up. After I got the tape out of the camera, I still could not get the tape to move in the cartridge when I activated the tape release, so it was really jammed in the cartridge with about five inches of tape hanging out.

On January 20, 2014, there was only a mild event; and it was maybe fifteen minutes before it stopped. On January 26, 2014, I set up the camcorder again; but the only thing it showed was that I snore loudly and move around a lot. No wonder Gloria has chosen to continue to sleep in another room!

There was some little stuff floating around at the beginning of the video that I suspect was dust out of focus going by the lens. There was a very mild event that night. I saw nothing unusual in the room, on the bed, or floating around. After this, there were some events every night but nothing different about them worth writing about.

On February 11, 2014, I felt a presence when I brushed my teeth and there seemed to be temperature change from cold to warm; and because my ears popped, I think there were pressure changes in the room. I saw nothing unusual around me or in the mirror. I was getting so used to having these events occur that now I'm just curious about what or who it was that caused it all.

There were two more intense events in which the pressure on top of me seemed higher, something was touching my face, and there was movement in my hair. The weight, I would guess, felt like fifteen to twenty pounds or so on top of my upper body. The first event happened on February 16, 2014. I actually struggled a bit to move against the weight that seemed to be holding me down, so I got up and checked myself out like I did the first time all this started to happen, worrying I may be having that stroke.

On February 24, 2014, it happened again with the weight. I tried to ignore it, then it all seemed to subside. Since this, I have sometimes felt a presence in the bedroom, but nothing seems to be happening like I have described anymore. I told Gloria, Phyllis, and Mina about it recently because if this ever gets published, they will read about it anyway. I didn't tell them about it while it was happening because I didn't want to freak them out. At first, I was freaked out enough for all of us!

When I think about smelling hot metal and gun smoke or gunpowder, I am reminded that astronauts say this is "the smell of space" they smell when they come back from a space walk. I suspect that it is caused by the radiation and particles from the sun that reacts with the material of their space suits, or even particles embedded in the space suit material. There is no way you can smell space since you need air to smell anything.

I have often had dreams about ghosts and the house being haunted, but now I am not so sure they were just dreams and may have been communication with spirits that are always around us. I very often have feelings there is someone around I can't see, and sometimes see movement or shadows out of the corner of my eye. As an engineer who always wants things to be measurable, explainable, and accurate as I can make them, I never expected to be writing what I have just written.

After I explain what I think we really are, I speculate about what may have actually happened.

16

Parade of Faces

About the time I started to think about writing a book sometime in 2015 (see how fast I worked on this), another strange thing happened. Some nights, for about a week, with my eyes closed just before falling asleep, I saw a face appear for a few moments, then another and another, both male and female—a parade of about thirty to forty faces, all different. I did not recognize any of them, but the sight was very vivid.

It was strange but stranger still was I was not startled by the sight. I just watched it all happen with my eyes still closed, wondering why I was seeing them. And then after it stopped, I fell asleep. I had no fear or any real reaction to the event, just curiosity about why it was happening. I didn't think I was going insane or anything like I had about some of the other experiences I had had. So I generated some questions about what it was as usual.

Was I seeing myself as I had looked in previous incarnations? I don't remember any of the men having beards, nor did the women have hair that appeared like it was from some other period in history. They all seemed to be contemporary faces. Was I seeing people I had associated with in a previous incarnation? Maybe not since I didn't recognize any of them, or did I not remember them for the same reason that has to do with not remembering previous lives?

Are they persons with whom I have to or had to work out karma? Are they people I will see in the future? If any of these, I probably wouldn't recognize them now even if I saw them again. All in all, there were hundreds of faces, and I don't think any of them were repeated. Are they people who have watched over me and helped me make decisions by influencing my dreams or something like that?

Are they advanced souls waiting for me to advance to their level? Do I have anything in common with these people? I may never know why I saw them unless there is some revelation given to me before I finish this life, or maybe they have told me in dreams and I will remember when something triggers the memory of why I have seen them.

Maybe they are people who are going to read this book if it ever gets published!

Recently, I had a somewhat interesting experience. I have to use eye drops to keep my eye pressure within normal limits—a drop in my left eye in the morning and a different medication in both eyes at bedtime. On August 21, 2020, and while I am writing this was yesterday, I was reclined in my reclining chair after putting the morning drop in my left eye. With both eyes closed, I saw the figure of a woman suddenly appear in front of me, stare at me for a few seconds, and then fade away.

This sort of thing has happened a few times before with different people appearing, and I don't completely recognize the people, maybe because they have changed so much if I knew them. I had no idea who it could be when it happened; however, she looked vaguely familiar. Thinking later it may be my sister-in-law Myra, who passed on August 1, I asked my sister Margaret if she had a recent picture of her; but she said she didn't.

When I called Marcia, she said she would send a copy of the obituary. She sent that with a copy of a candid unposed picture I had given her that I took of Myra with others in the family when we all got together in North Dakota several years ago. Now that I have seen the picture on the obituary, I am sure it was her. There was some resemblance to the picture I had taken, while the resemblance to the obituary picture, except for being black and white, was the apparition I saw.

Now I wonder how long she had been there. Was she there for a while before I saw the apparition and still there after I saw her fade away, and if she was, why did she appear to fade away? I wonder what she saw when she was looking at me. Did I appear to fade away to her or did she actually just leave? If she left, how did she leave? I didn't see her make a move to leave.

I speculate about soul-to-soul communication later (next chapter actually), and that may be how we saw each other. After all, I did see her with my eyes closed, and I didn't open them when I saw her. I wonder if I would have seen her if I had my eyes open at the time. She sure didn't stay long, but that creates another question for me. How long was that moment in the universe she occupied at that moment I saw her? I speculate about that later too.

I had similarly seen a few of my brothers and sisters who had passed on, but at the time, the visions happened I thought it was just a momentary memory I had of them. I had seen Lynn in a dream, and as I was slowly waking up, he appeared to slowly recede into the distance, then disappear. I didn't know if I moved away from him or he was moving away from me. I think it was the former because he seemed to be sitting in a chair when I saw him.

Because of the fact I didn't know for sure the entity I saw was Myra, until I saw her picture as she appeared just before she passed proved to me, I was actually seeing her spirit, not a memory; therefore, I was probably seeing family members as spirits too. But I still puzzle over seeing all those faces one after the other. What could that possibly have been?

17

Some Conclusions and/or Questions

My life has been total chaos with all the weird stuff happening all around me, to me, and seems to have guided me all the way to at least today by things I hadn't understood. Now, I have theorized several explanations which I hope could clarify my life somewhat. Don't get me wrong; I don't pretend to have all the answers or to be totally convinced about what I am going to write. It's just that I can think of no other explanations for the direction I have taken, the things I have experienced, and the effect it has had on me and those around me. I am probably going to generate many more questions than I have any speculative answers to.

I believe in reincarnation and karma. Why? Because no one could get this screwed up in one lifetime! Well maybe that's not true. Look at some of the people in government. Oh wait, they may have lived several lifetimes too. I believe in karma because it makes everything fair. By that, I am referring to the different conditions people are born into. How can having serious illness all your life be fair? How could slavery have been fair at all? What causes some people to treat others so badly and seem to get away with it? Why are some people born into wealth while some can't seem to ever have enough?

I believe in reincarnation and karma, and I think the people I have in my life are part of that. Why else was my life directed to the person I married in such subtle and not so subtle ways by something I didn't seem to have control over? Even dreaming Gloria's name and of the things we may be planning for the weekend was weird. Why was I so interested in the dog in the encyclopedia I was almost obsessed with as a kid even though I didn't like dogs?

The darn things were always putting their noses where they don't belong, the horny devils. Some of them bite without provocation. I believe we preexisted this life in some other form in another kind of matter, have transitioned into this existence, and occupied these bodies for some purpose. We just don't know or can't remember what that purpose is, at least we don't know while we occupy these bodies. Maybe there are some people who remember all of it and know our purpose here, but I am not one of them. I believe that Jesus *was* one of them.

I know our souls are real, having seen them, and I think that they existed somewhere and somehow a long time before our current lives and that they enter us or start to influence us at birth. I wonder if they are in or influencing us before we are born because that would seem to be in conflict and cause confusion with the mom's spirit. Maybe that would explain the strange mood swings associated with pregnancy, so maybe they are in the action already. Okay, so another question unanswered. Don't worry because I have lots more of them to not answer. Like I said, I don't pretend to have the answers, but I can generate questions like mad!

I believe that most imaginary friends we all seem to have as children are not imaginary but are other souls. I believe souls, either incarnate or discarnate, communicate with each other, if not constantly then quite often. When our souls enter our body, I think our brain has a close connection to it and can communicate with and through the soul and can communicate with other like souls and know they can, at least for about the first five years of our lives.

Why such a short time? It's because communicating with and through souls isn't the primary job of our brains. Our brains first must learn to deal with the flesh, bone, and blood thing it is part of. It has to process the five senses (or more) and learn how to move the muscles to move the bones; balance the body on two feet; move the feet to make it walk, sit down, stand up, run, jump; learn to speak;

learn about the world to recognize everything and everybody around it; and so much more.

At about five years old, our brains have become really good at a lot of that stuff, but it has lost the capability of communicating directly with the soul and therefore with other souls it had known so well. The only spirit communication it has not lost is when it can quiet the body that it must control during sleep or meditation (which I could never seem to purposely do because I try to analyze everything) or when the body is in a relaxed state where the world seems to disappear and then the soul "talks to it and through it."

I believe we dream every important event in our lives before we live them, or in other words, we predict the future. How is that possible? How can a person dream the future? I'll just have to try to explain what I think about that later when I write about how I think our universe is constructed.

Sorry about repeating stuff, but I believe ghosts or spirits are real and I have seen some of them so I am quite sure that it is a fact. I know they were there and were spirits because of the fact they disappeared (at least to my eyes) and I could no longer see them. Most people are incapable of just disappearing. I will not say no one can just disappear because, at this point, nothing would surprise me.

I am puzzled over why I was able to see them at times and then couldn't though. Where did the light that accompanied one of them go? Was it the building lights I saw, or was there a light that surrounded the entity I saw? Did he bring the light with him, or did he actually use light switches? And if he used light switches, how did he turn them off so fast after I saw him in the light?

It was a matter of moments between when I saw him at the desk and then the dark room with him not visible. Did my realizing he should not be there cause me not see him even though he was still there, or was he really not there anymore? How can we feel the presence of a spirit and not see them? Can we see them unconsciously with it not registering completely in the brain, or does the soul perceive them and only leave a hint that they are there to our brain? Why do so many people report seeing a hazy cloud, shadow, or indistinct ghost when the ones I saw looked as solid as another "live human being?

Many others have seen them as a solid human being would look to their eyes. The only way I could tell they were spirits was when they disappeared or seemed to disappear. Of course, there have been a lot of people reporting seeing a person who then disappears are able to describe the person and have reported seeing the same entity as others. My son and I seeing the same one at the same time is a good example of that.

Experiencing what I have and reading about and seeing psychics on TV, I know we coexist with spirits or ghosts here on earth. Reading about what scientists have theorized about the universe, I have also theorized what this universe is like in the following chapters. We know that neither religion nor science seem to have solved the riddles of reality and in fact raise more questions the more we learn, so I decided that I should create even more questions.

Death, I know, is not the end of us because I have seen entities who are supposed to be dead look to be very much alive in some form. I still puzzle over what state I am in when I saw them because, in at least one case, I was very tired having had to get up at 0-dark hundred to go to work to support operations, half-asleep in a hurry to get to the bathroom; and at other times, I was very much awake and driving or talking to a very attractive young lady while I waited to talk to someone else.

There was no pattern to my seeing them. I have written about ones I knew for sure had actually happened. There were numerous times I had seen people on the street and I wondered where they went suddenly. Until I thought more about the events I have described, I didn't think that much about them, but now, I realize that it may have been happening to me a lot over the years.

I think a medium is a person who still has some soul-brain connection that is active throughout their lives and is not totally lost when the brain has to deal with life experiences. They still have to quiet the body some to allow the connection to be active though. Having the soul being able to communicate with the brain and also other spirits or souls allows them to relay information from "the beyond" or whatever you think of it as. Maybe you think of it as baloney, but I believe they have maintained at least a little more soul-brain connection than most people and actually communicate with discarnate spirits. I believe that is what a psychic is and does.

As people enter the terminal phases of their lives, I believe that the soul-brain connection starts to return for at least some of us, if not for all of us. Gloria's dad said there were dead people in the back-yard as he was getting weaker toward the end of his life. Maybe this is because the nerve, muscle connections, thinking, and sensing in the body returned to levels nearer to what it was as a child, while the soul-brain connection strengthens.

My ninety-five-year-old brother, who recently passed away, when he was getting weaker, said that he goes into the hills and talks to God. I believe his soul was actually communicating with someone he believed was God, and maybe it was. Whoever he talked to I am sure exists in some universe separate but coincident with this one. Later, I'll explain how I think that to be true. But what do I know? I'm an engineer, not a doctor or psychiatrist. Oh wait, maybe that is an asset that qualifies me to make these conclusions!

What about a composer who goes to sleep one night and in the morning wakes up with a complete musical composition in his head, or Mozart playing the piano at age three and composing music at age four? I believe these are souls communicating with their brains. They dream the future and have some kind of memory of it. Maybe they didn't have time in a previous life to compose what they wanted and are now able to do it in this life but do it at a very young age before the brain gets too busy. They then continue to create great music compositions throughout their lives, possibly because of what they did as young children that made their brain work that way.

What about the person you just thought of calls you on the phone or a short time later knocks on your door? It's a dream come true like ones I had before. Somehow, something that was put in your brain got triggered at the right time by another thought or the time it was supposed to happen arrived to trigger the "memory." Or maybe it is soul-to-soul communication just before it happens.

Time does not seem to enter the picture when it comes to prophesy and dreaming the future. The future must exist for us to be able to receive information about it because there would be no way it could be generated in our perception otherwise. Where would the information come from if it doesn't exist somehow and somewhere? I will attempt an answer to that too.

My life, my fault, or maybe my soul's fault

I speculated on why so many of the women I almost associated with couldn't or wouldn't carry on a conversation and seemed to have no interest in me. My theory is, as I said earlier, that souls somehow always communicate with each other even when they are incarnated. The whole thing was a plot cooked up by my soul, my scheming soul, to keep me on the straight-and-narrow path that took me to what I am now in this life and to not deviate from the path it had set for me.

Karma must have played a big role in it all, and my soul made darn sure that I stayed on the path to the goal, whatever that is now. I don't have the foggiest notion of what the ultimate goal was or is and will probably never know while I am in this body, and I guess that is how it has to be. Since we all can't remember previous incarnations, we can't see what karma we have built up, but the soul knows it all and tries to clean up the messes we have made. How did mine do that?

Every time a nice-looking woman came around the soul conversation may have gone something like this.

My brain says, "Wow, that's nice."

Then my soul says to my brain, "Take it easy. She is not interested in you. Why should she be? You're not that great."

Her soul may have said, "He seems to like my host and she likes him too, so maybe they should get to know each other."

My soul probably replied with something like, "Oh no you don't. He is off limits. You have to make her too shy to even talk to him."

"But she really likes him."

"Too bad because I created a plan for him and he has to follow it.

"Why can't they get together, at least get to know each other and maybe have some fun?"

"Because he had too much fun in his previous lives and has lots of karma to fix."

"Darn it. You are a spoilsport, a real killjoy!"

"He has got to stick to the plan. Now leave him alone."

I'm sure my soul thought to itself or maybe even talked to itself as well, but it probably didn't blush when it did that. The dialogue maybe was something like this.

Note to soul self: "Okay, soul self, don't forget you have to keep this guy shy so he doesn't get too frisky! Let's see what else should I do? Oh yeah, make him kind of freak out about his caved-in chest and the fact he is a ninety-seven-pound weakling like in Joe's ads so whenever he gets in a position where he likes a girl, he keeps thinking he isn't worthy of her. Make him think he could never be the He-Man he thinks she must be attracted to. Make him do or say something stupid that messes up any relationship that may accidently have been formed. These rules don't apply when he meets the Gloria he is supposed to meet, but they do apply to other women as long as he lives!"

So now some readers (if there are any) are thinking the guy who wrote this is out of his mind. Insanity certainly reigns where he is, and his mom was so right when she said that. Maybe you just think I am nuts or I am just kidding about the whole thing. So my challenge to anyone who thinks so is to explain "He is the only man I ever met I don't know what to say to."

While I was rereading what I had written and made some changes that I hoped would clarify some of the mess I had written, another thought occurred to me. If I had control over my own soul, then maybe I could influence how it communicated with other souls and get their hosts to do things I wanted them to do. Maybe that is how some people are able to influence others, but I'm not able to do that. I really think it was my soul all the time causing me and those I met to do what it wanted. I'm a slave or a robot to my soul!

18

What I Think Scientists Think about the Universe

Mathematicians, physicists, and scientists are trying to describe the universe and solve its mysteries and figure out why it operates the way it does. There have been many theories about what matter consists of and to explain why energy interacts with matter as it does. The theories can only go so far to explain what everything is and why.

Giant atom smashers have been built to study elementary particles of which everything is made. Weird things have been seen and created in these devices, and not all the experts can agree on what they have really seen. But the following may be close to the consensus of many of them. The terminology used to describe the basic particles for matter and energy is the fault of those experts. I will add to the terminology later, but let us see what they have come up with first (at least what I think they have come up with). I will only describe this stuff as I misunderstand it!

As human beings, we consist of molecules which consist of atoms which consist of protons and neutrons (which consist of quarks of various "flavors" and "colors") and electrons and positrons. Quarks come in six "flavors"—up, down, strange, charmed, bottom and top—and in three "colors": red, blue, and green. Also, there are other sets that are antiquarks with the same names, only they are in anticolors. I didn't make this up, so I am not to blame for the terminology. But it looks kind of cute!

I wonder sometimes if someone's kid came up with the terminology. Then to confuse things a bit more, scientists have three categories called bosons which carry force (mesons, photons, gluons, and maybe gravitons if they exist) which make up the four forces: gravity, electromagnetism, strong interaction, and weak interaction; fermions making up matter, which include leptons, quarks, electrons, neutrinos, and baryons; and sort of overlapping them both are hadrons. These things have different spin, and some of them have to spin twice to come up with a complete revolution (if that's what it is), or in other words, to go back to the original state! There are a few more things thrown in to make thirty-eight or more elementary particles that make up the stuff we and our universe are made of, which is enough to make you crazy-ons!

There are also energies that are totally invisible to us but also electromagnetic energy at a frequency we can see but only as a reflection off something or when we look directly at the source (not advisable in the case of the sun) and enter directly into our eyes. If we could see energy at a wavelength at the level of quark size, we would see that atoms are very nearly empty space, but of course, that is impossible for us to see. Also, light appears to be both particles and waves simultaneously because sometimes it acts like waves, sometimes like particles, and is in little chunks called photons.

We know this because when energy is supplied to an atom, electrons move within the atom to a higher energy state and absorb a photon with a certain amount of energy and when the electron drops back to the lower energy state, it emits a photon with that same energy (and color, by the way). Scientists and mathematicians don't like anything simple, or is it that nothing is simple and they only discover it's not simple?

Every second of our lives, we also have millions of neutrinos passing through our bodies completely unnoticed. Neutrinos have very little mass, if any; and we can't see them, taste them, feel them, or do anything with them. The only way they can be detected is when they interact with some other particle that generates energy we can see. They come from our sun and from other stars around us, but you would never know they are there except that scientists tell you they are there.

They are so elusive that it takes a special detector to see them at all and then the number that can be detected of the billions of them is really small. Scientists actually took a neutrino picture of the sun, which was kind of unusual in that the picture was taken at night! The neutrino camera "saw" the sun through the earth, so the neutrinos that made the picture passed through the earth, probably interacting with only a few atoms of the earth and maybe some of those are what was detected. The device is a huge tank of water with particle detectors in it that detect particles driven off atoms in the water. It took several nights to catch enough particles to make the picture because so few neutrinos caused any reactions.

If you turn on a radio or television, you can hear and see many different stations transmitting electromagnetic signals of various frequencies, of various formats, and of various powers. There are also communication systems all over the planet allowing people to communicate with each other and space vehicles transmitting a bunch of data, so there are millions of signals almost everywhere. Some of those signals are very strong and some are very weak. You cannot detect the signals to see them or hear them without a receiver. There is no way that you could know they were there without such devices to receive the signals.

Turn on a microwave oven, and you can cook food with the microwave energy you can't see. But you know something happened because the food gets hot. X-rays pass through your body and do so without giving you any feeling that anything happened, but you can see your bones on the computer screen or X-ray picture so you know that it happened when someone took your X-ray.

Space is full of energy called cosmic rays that never reach the surface of the earth because they are blocked by the atmosphere. You can see the results of cosmic rays when they collide with the atmospheric gases because a shower of charged particles is released, some of which can be seen as condensation trails in cloud chambers or be detected in some other detection devices. The effects of showers of charged particles emitted from the sun can be seen as the aurora in the north and south when gases in our atmosphere are ionized by the particles and the gasses emit photons.

Aurora only occur near the poles (magnetic poles actually) because the particles follow the magnetic field of the earth, which is also invisible to us and you can't feel it either. You can see the effects of the magnetic field with a compass or feel a magnetic force when you have a magnet and something that can be magnetized like iron.

Air is a good example of matter that exists right around us that we can't see directly. We only see blue sky because the air scatters blue light and you can't see the water vapor in the air unless there is a lot of it, then it appears hazy and, when it cools, forms clouds. But we can feel the effects of air when the wind blows, so we have no doubt it is there. Also, if you haven't noticed before, it's what you've been breathing all this time!

Every square inch of your body has approximately 14.7 pounds of air pressure on it, and depending on how big you are, you could have anywhere from thirty thousand to fifty thousand pounds or more total pressure on your skin surface and you don't feel it at all. Lakes are full of water that, at some places, is almost invisible. You can see clearly pebbles and sand at the bottom of the lake. And of course, seen at an angle, the water surface reflects whatever is around it like hills and trees which, when reflected, you see on the water upside down.

There appear to be massive particles that exist that interact with other particles very weakly and are called weakly interacting massive particles (WIMPs). Scientists don't know exactly what they are but think they explain what they call dark matter, and they are accompanied by undetectable energy they call dark energy. And it appears there is a lot more of that than there is matter and energy we can detect.

Scientists are trying to figure out why galaxies rotate the way they do, so they have hypothesized that there is dark energy and matter that we can't see that adds gravity to the galaxies. Gravity is considered a weak force, and it is thought that all the particles do interact gravitationally. If neutrinos had enough mass, they could be enough to fill in the dark matter sufficiently to explain the motion of the galaxies, but scientists don't think they do.

Scientists also speculate there are other weird particles that make up the constituents of our universe among which are narrow, long (comparatively) things called strings that help them explain some of the phenomenon they see in the universe and in experiments. As though it wasn't already complicated enough! So later on, I will reveal my ideas to make it seem even more complicated!

19

Multiverse or Polyverse

I am an electronics engineer, not a theoretical physicist or mathematician, so the following may be a bit unscholarly sounding. I hope I don't get so far into the weeds in what looks like nonsense or babbling that I appear to be what Mom said about insanity reigning where I am.

What I write in this chapter are conclusions I came to over a period of time, and several times, I woke up with some ideas and made a few notes when I actually had the presence of mind to have a tablet and pencil handy. Some of the ideas were based on books I read about psychics, spirits, and religion; but most of it is from thinking about all the weird stuff happening to me in the past seventy years or so.

I do not list reading sources in this book except for a very few of them because it is impossible for me to remember all of them. Stephen Hawking was one source (*A Brief History of Time*), and that is how I think I know what theoretical physicists are thinking lately about our universe, at least the part I think I understood. I read again recently (notice I did not say *learned*) about quarks, other particles, and dark matter in that book. I had also read some material from George Gamow way back in my ancient history as a teenager.

This is what I believe. We live in a universe within a system of universes, and it may be several layers of universes. Each one is built upon some basic building blocks that combine in certain ways to become matter that we are made of and that we can see, touch, and interact with. I think there are other building blocks (maybe the ones we consist of and interact with were made of but maybe totally different) forming matter and energy we cannot see and cannot interact with except maybe gravitationally, and I suspect some that doesn't even react gravitationally.

There could be another universe overlaying this one that is made up of building blocks that make up our quarks, mesons, bosons, energy, etc.; but they are assembled differently from basic building blocks to form that universe or totally different building blocks that may make up all the other universe(s). Those other universe particles and energy are made from other combinations of particles and energy we can't detect with our limited detection systems based on our electromagnetic devices and capabilities.

There are probably other forms of energy and particles between ours and whatever the basic ones consist of. There may be multiple universes layered one upon the other, including the one we inhabit, totally disconnected from each other except through the weak forces. Yes, I said that several ways on purpose. *Multi* is from Latin and *poly* is from Greek, and because most of what the scientists have theorized is Greek to me, I will choose the Greek version. I think it is actually a polyverse we live in, and I will call it that just to be different because others have used multiverse. But I think they are just thinking of many universes not necessarily on top of each other. From now on, I will call the polyverse (or system of universes) UNIVERSE with all capital letters.

I think we consist of nothing but WIMPs; and that has nothing to do with our character, our strength, or our bravery. We are a special group of particles that interact with each other to produce visible or detectable (to us) stellar systems, air, metals, rocks, dirt, chemicals, water, fruits, vegetables, trees, animals, insects, and human beings but that there are a lot more particles and energy we don't react with except weakly and that we cannot detect, see, taste, smell or feel.

But remember that all the matter we see is mostly empty space; the ones we can't see are also mostly empty space, and there are particles passing right through it all no matter what it is. What we see as solid steel, lead, and uranium are far from solid; and these other particles pass through them, as well as us, the earth, and all we can see as though our stuff doesn't even exist.

That is what I think the other universes within the UNIVERSE are all doing, passing right through all that we see and can't see and each other in our universe. We are currently stuck in a limited part of all that exists. The rest of the UNIVERSE is blocked from our perception by the limited perception range of our bodies and the limits of the physics available to us to build anything to enable us to see outside of our limited universe. Some of us may have some limited capability to perceive (mostly only momentary) glimpses of other universes via the inner being we each carry, which I will attempt to explain my theories on later (or at least create more questions about).

Currently, scientists are trying their best to find the so-called dark matter and dark energy which are probably the other part of the UNIVERSE and, except for gravitational effects, probably undetectable to us because of the limits of the equipment that can be created with our limited universe constituents. To build detectors that could show us properties of the other universes, we would probably need some of whatever constitutes other parts of the UNIVERSE, if we could figure out what that was.

But if we could get those constituents, we wouldn't need to detect them anymore! That is kind of like looking for the cows. Don't look for them anymore after you find them, except in this case, we would maybe want to study the material! There are forms of matter and energy we can't even conceive of. Actually, there is matter and energy in *our* universe we can't conceive of.

To illustrate what I think the UNIVERSE is like, imagine an orchestra consisting of humans, dogs, bats, whales, porpoises, and dolphins and each having instruments or internal instruments that play near the limits of sounds they can hear. Each unique note would be like an element, each chord would be like a molecule of different elements. They could all be playing the same composition in their upper and lower registers, and we would only be able to hear about 45 to 19,000 Hz notes so we would hear only a very limited amount of the total composition.

The dogs would hear up to 45,000 Hz; some bats up to 90,000 Hz and others up to 180,000 Hz; porpoises and dolphins would hear up to 150,000 Hz; and whales are playing real low down to maybe 14 Hz. But it could all be there at the same time. In other words, they could all be playing the same notes but in different octaves. Our hearing apparatus would not even know that the lowest- and highest-pitched instruments were playing at all. Now this is kind of a lame example of what I think the UNIVERSE is like. You kind of have to imagine the sounds in totally different ways to include both matter and energy.

I thought of another lame example. Chocolate cake batter consists of flour, eggs, water, sugar, oil, salt, baking soda (I think), maybe some vanilla, and cocoa. When it is all mixed together, it really only looks like chocolate color stuff and you can't see the rest of the ingredients so you just think chocolate cake batter. The water, eggs, and other ingredients are no longer visible or look very different. A particle of flour may still appear as a particle of flour, or some egg may still appear like egg to microbes that are on or in them. Each ingredient represents a universe, and combined, they are the UNIVERSE. Oh man (or woman or whatever—can't be sexist) that is so lame!

I believe that there are different rules for the various universes in the UNIVERSE. We in this universe have time and space and a speed limit that is the speed of light, which is pretty fast at about 186,000 miles per second. No physical matter we are familiar with can move at a speed beyond the speed of light, and strange things happen to that matter near that speed. The mass of matter approaching that speed increases drastically toward infinite mass. Time on anything approaching the speed of light also slows down according to Einstein's theory of relativity. In addition to the speed limit, we can only experience this universe in one direction. The past is the past, the present is happening, and the future hasn't happened yet as far as we and our normal senses and memories are concerned.

Where does the information about the future come from that I have seemed to tap into from time to time and that others seem to do also? For someone to access information about the future, the future has to exist already. I believe there is a universe in the UNIVERSE that has no speed limit at all. In fact, time does not exist; and the past, present, and future all exist simultaneously and there is simply *now*.

It is a part of and *as big as* the huge UNIVERSE, but time and distance mean nothing. And with no time and distance constraints, the inhabitants of that universe can be anywhere or everywhere now. That *now* universe, the primary one, contains all that happened, is happening, and ever will happen. That, I think, is the universe we (our spirits) are from originally; and that is how, when or if we can contact that universe, the future here in our currently occupied universe can be predicted by us as souls or spirits or maybe our spirits already know the information.

We as human beings can know things from that universe in our brains if it can communicate with the spirit. Our spirits, the real us, may have transitioned through different levels of universes to get here. What did Jesus mean when he said, "In my father's house there are many mansions"? Is that different levels of universe within the UNIVERSE? Or is that something completely different? If that all sounds confusing, think about the concepts *forever* or *nothing ever existing*.

I can't conceive of those concepts. I don't think anyone else can either, and because of what we are experiencing, we tend to think there has to be some beginning and ending. We know we exist now, or at least we think we do. It is actually easier to think of an all-encompassing *now* with past, present, and future all in one. Then there is no forever, or everything beginning or ceasing to exist, but just *now*. Okay, so maybe that isn't easier. But it is interesting!

In this and the following paragraphs, I am not trying to argue with scientists or mathematicians even though they don't all agree with each other. What was the big bang that created our universe? I'm thinking the big bang may have happened in the primary UNIVERSE, which already existed, as a temporary expansion of a different kind of mass and energy; and the very basic constituents of that universe were converted to constituents of our universe as the motion slowed to less than our light speed.

Otherwise, the big bang would have disobeyed our speed limit by a lot! Of course, scientists say that the entire universe itself inflated rapidly so no speed limits were disobeyed as all space expanded. So how do they know that if they can only detect about a tenth of all that exists? Is our universe really expanding at an increasing rate as scientists think it is?

I don't think we know where we are in the universe, so no matter which direction we look, the galaxies seem to be moving away at the same distances at the same rates (unless I misunderstand that). If we are in an expanding universe, shouldn't it depend on where we are in the universe as to how fast they seem to move away in different directions? Or maybe because the universe is so large that in our part of it, you cannot discern the difference in speed each direction. We can't really tell.

Thinking more about the universe expanding at an ever-increasing rate, is that really what we are seeing when we see deeper into space and back in time or are we seeing a universe that is really slowing down but having been expanding faster in the past? We would necessarily see galaxies moving away faster billions of light years away because they were moving away faster billions of years in the past.

It is a bit confusing when scientists say things far away *are* accelerating when they are seeing things that happened way back *in the past*. Maybe they are really seeing the remnants of the inflationary period as it slowed. Therefore, the further away (and further in the past), we are simply seeing the motion that is the remnants of the inflationary period for our visible universe. Maybe our universe is not yet as big as the UNIVERSE.

After I had written the paragraphs above, I also reread *A Brief History of Time* and another Hawking book called *The Universe in a Nutshell* (I recently bought both books in one volume) in which Hawking had speculated that there may be others in the universe (UNIVERSE) of other types of matter who are looking for their universes missing mass, of which we are a part of course. That's what I am getting at in this book.

I also speculate about a part of us in another form of matter that appear to us as ghosts which some of us we can somehow see, even though we are in our present form. Some see them as shadows, some as indistinct cloudy figures, some as a glowing orb, or as I saw them, looking as solid (but mostly empty space of course) as us.

I think one of us in another form passed through my body as I wrote about earlier and caused me to think I was the one who was dead. Having a dead body in this world doesn't stop us from being alive in some other form in another part of the UNIVERSE and still hanging around thinking we are still alive in this universe. Somehow, that form is able to interact with us in what we have been calling spirit form.

In their universe, they probably appear as solid as we appear in ours. But probably, they are also limited in seeing and experiencing as we are in our present universe, so maybe most of the time, they couldn't see us at all. Maybe the one who passed through me did see me but was too late to step aside. I will probably not know while I am in my present life. I believe an occupant in any universe within the UNIVERSE who has reached the *ultimate level of knowledge and perfection*—if that is our ultimate goal—is free to occupy any of the universes at will and can manipulate the matter and energy in them either advertently or inadvertently and can intervene or help another entity in them.

I am really curious about what the other universes are like. Do they add dimensions or contain completely different ones? How many different universes are in the UNIVERSE? Are the other universes multidimensional or nondimensional? Can they even be described using our limited vocabulary?

Even though I may sound like I am making fun of what scientists have come up with (some are quite funny), I really respect the efforts they have made in trying to describe what may be indescribable in any language we are familiar with: physics, mathematics, and what have you. I think they are dealing with the indescribable but amazing UNIVERSE in which we live that, speaking as though time really exists in the UNIVERSE, we may understand one day.

20

Psychic Experience or What Really Happens?

Many people don't believe in psychics at all even if they have had what can only be described as psychic experiences. I would probably have been one of them, since I was so interested in science until the weird things I have described started to happen when I was young. What I now believe, I shall try to explain how I think psychics get the information they get, what they get, and how some of the information is used.

I believe we all have a spirit or soul, the same as most of the population of the earth believe. I also believe that our souls were around for a very long time as time exists in our universe. I believe that, somehow, we came from a primary universe separate but coincidental to this one. In other words, other spirits are currently around us totally unseen and totally involved in whatever they have going on. They may or may not be involved with us unless we need help (my mom calling my name for instance).

To some of those spirits, everything is simply happening now as time does not exist for them depending on what level they are on. They can be involved in anything, anywhere, anytime, anyhow, and may be simultaneously in other universes in which time exists. Where time exists, everything happens in sequence, but where time does not exist, everything is just happening. Are there universes where time is reversed? Since the UNIVERSE contains all the universes, with or without time, I will just use the word UNIVERSE for where information of past, present, and future is obtained since it also has to be timeless. Remember that all I write about is what *I believe* to be true.

All children under about age five have less limitations in their perception than we all do after that age. A newborn baby has no control over its body except for a few things such as suckling, which was learned in the womb. That baby is closer to "seeing" the UNIVERSE as it really is than any of us because the soul can have a direct influence on the brain.

The first thing a baby brain has to do to control a functioning human body is to adapt to the body nerve system and learn to control muscles and interpret the five or more sensory inputs. As the control of the body is advanced in controlling balance, walking, talking, learning, and dealing with life experience and as this "learning" fills our brains with so called facts, the perception range decreases as physical life "takes over" our being.

I think imaginary friends are not imaginary but are as real as we are. That is why my daughter could talk to Dad years after he died. They tend to disappear from our perception as our brains get more involved with physical life and all the learning it has to do, and then it loses the connection with the soul. We are then as limited to our body's senses as we ever get except when we have momentary expanded perception through dreams, meditation, etc. There are exceptions of various degrees of course, and those are called psychics.

Our inner being (spirit or soul) is freer to experience beyond the limitations of our universe during sleep, when we are very relaxed as during meditation or when it is important for us to be aware (as in saving our lives or something like that). It is what causes some people who are somewhat psychic to change things they do every day, like help with the kids instead of going to work and miss being killed (like in the Twin Towers) or without knowing why they slam on the brakes just short of a cliff instead of driving into a river and remain alive. If the inner being has decided it is time to return to that part of the UNIVERSE where it is meant to return, then your physical body will die by accident if necessary for that to happen.

We have dreamed our future, and we do whatever it takes to accomplish our dreams almost as a slave to our inner being. Our inner being is capable of allowing us to actually see departed beings for a short while. A psychic is able to control the body in some way so that the connection of the soul to the UNIVERSE is strengthened and information extracted from any of the universes or other souls can communicate with it. This can be accomplished by actually going into a trance like Edgar Cayce did or by scribbling on a tablet of paper like the Hollywood Medium does or simply sleeping, whatever tends to quiet the body or enter a trance state so the soul can contact "home."

There are some who have a constant connection and can or have to ignore it unless it demands attention. I believe that Jesus's soul had a constant communication with the UNIVERSE and his brain. He was totally aware of where we came from and what and where we will be once again. I think he tried to communicate that to his disciples but totally confused them instead because they couldn't conceive of anything out of this world. If you wonder who Edgar Cayce was, there are books written about him such as *Edgar Cayce, The Sleeping Prophet* by Jess Stearn and *There Is a River* by Thomas Sugrue, which were among the first of many that I have read.

If all the various universes are piled on top of each other, psychics should be able to access any one of them to extract information and maybe even to see the beings that populate those universes if they can quiet the body enough to allow spirit to brain communication again. But then, I think about the fact that various ones I saw did not depend on me actually quieting my body at all.

I was very busy when I saw them so that is a bit confusing, but maybe that is because I am a bit more psychic. Some psychics would be less limited by the brain-body limitations and could perceive things others would not be able to during normal daily living. I guess I am one of them, but I have no control over when it is active or over what information I get. What happens to me just happens without my having any influence over it.

When we as psychics see a discarnate spirit with our eyes, what are we actually seeing? Does the spirit carry some of the particles of matter from our universe that we see and our soul/brain connection fill in the missing matter so we see a whole ghost of that person, or do we actually see into the universe they actually inhabit and see them as they exist in that universe?

Are they temporarily in between the different types of matter of the two universes and carry some of the matter of both or is it totally our psychic vision that enables us to see them in their new form? I think it is likely the latter and they are still hanging around where we can see them. There may be some people among us who can see into the other universes temporarily, but that would be rare.

It may have happened to me momentarily, but I am still not sure I really saw what thought I saw. Is that what Buddhists call enlightenment? Since the universes are all coincident with each other in the UNIVERSE, the discarnate spirit is in the same realm as us even though occupying another universe in different forms of matter and energy. If we could see into their universe, wouldn't we see their universe instead of just them seeming to still be with us in our universe? Even in their new (or is it former) form, they may think they still occupy this universe and are still interacting with it.

When we sleep, I believe we dream life-changing or important events in our lives before they happen, which probably prepares us for them. I think we dream a lot of unimportant events before they occur too. Much of the déjà vu we experience is quite unimportant. How do we do it? During sleep, the soul is very busy gathering information from the UNIVERSE—where the past, present, and future all exist—about the future events and creating the dreams to put the information in our brains.

We don't usually remember them until the conditions occur that trigger the memory or the fight/flight response because the memory is not a normal experience memory but is put in our brains via the soul. Something in the dream sequence must occur in our physical lives to trigger the memory. Something simple, like a change in road noise or a pattern in the road crack patches, for example, triggered a reaction to an imbedded memory, causing the extreme panic I had, from what I didn't even know until I was looking over the precipice at the barricade with the flashing lights below me.

I still shudder when I think about the disaster that could have occurred except for a soul dream buried deeply in my brain. It also can explain the person I married, the delay going to RTMC, flipping the wrong light switch and falling on my face, and a bunch of other events in my life. I somehow reacted to or "remembered the future events memory" my soul put in my brain and acted on the information to accomplish whatever needed to be accomplished at the time.

Why and how did I hear Mom calling my nickname to avoid a car crash? I've come up with a few explanations of how that could come about because I really don't know for sure what happened; I just know it did and I can't forget it. Maybe I had a prophetic memory implanted in my brain by my soul and something triggered the dream/memory sequence. My mind then reconstructed the memory of how she said my nickname, and I heard it in my mind as an auditory phenomenon that really didn't happen outside of my brain. Maybe Mom's soul saw the impending disaster and warned my soul of what was about to happen, and to wake me up quickly, my soul caused my brain to remember how she said my nickname and my brain then reconstructed the sound again as an auditory phenomenon that didn't happen outside of my brain.

Maybe Mom's soul saw the impending disaster and warned my soul of what was about to happen, and to wake me up quickly, my soul triggered my brain to use my own voice modified to sound like I remembered Mom's voice to say my nickname. Maybe Mom's soul was with me on the trip home, and when she saw the impending crash, she actually manipulated matter in this universe to recreate the sound of her voice saying my nickname the way she always said it. I think it was the latter explanation because I think departed souls are around us all the time. Whatever way this happened, it was very effective because I was so fully awake immediately after it happened that I wouldn't have fallen asleep again even if I hadn't stopped to get some fresh air.

What actually happened in my haunted bedroom? Possibly a lady who had an interest in me passed away, and thinking she was still alive, her soul was actually in my bedroom and I felt her presence in the bed. That may have happened a few times, and it had freaked me out a bit. Other times, I was not concerned at all when I felt a presence, which seemed a bit odd at the time.

I asked Gloria if she had dreamed that she was sleeping back in our bedroom, and she said she had several times. I have concluded that it was her most of the time and another lady sometimes. Gloria said she thought she knew exactly who the other lady was, and when she told me, I was surprised to say the least.

She had an interest in me? I had said I think souls, or maybe a part of the soul, wander around at night when their host is sleeping, are free to do it any time when the host is dead of course, and that is how this happened. I have also dreamed we are together in bed again, and that is what gave me the clue that it could have been Gloria's soul most of the time.

Why do some people have an immediate attraction for each other even though they may not be what they think of as very attractive? I believe this must be communication at the soul level and they know each other well from being together many times in their past lives, even though they don't realize it when they meet; and later, without realizing how true it is, they may refer to each other as soul mates.

Before I saw the apparition of Myra, I didn't know how much she had aged or exactly what she looked like, and therefore, I could not have filled in the details that I saw as I had speculated about what we actually were seeing when we see a ghost. The apparition had to be complete somehow when I perceived it.

Her image had to somehow be impressed on my brain's visual center for me to see her as she actually appeared. It was not an actual visual phenomenon because my eyes were closed, so I believe it had to be a soul-to-soul communication. And her image was impressed on my brain similarly to how prophetic dreams are but as a visual image. Was she standing there several minutes of the time for her in this or the universe she was in, if not this one, or was it seconds like I saw her in the universe I am in? Or was she still occupying space in this universe as a spirit or some sort of energy and was really only there for a few seconds?

Time may be different in the universes that have time, and what seems like a second here may be quite different in another universe in which time exists. When we remember a dream of several minutes or even hours, we are really only dreaming a short time measured in seconds, so that shows our perception of time here is variable depending on what we are doing. We must have many dreams each night but only remember a few of them or even none of them in the morning. Many of those dreams are putting future memories into our brains.

Speaking of time, it seems to speed up as we age, and the years start whizzing by so fast that we hardly have time to get used to the new year before it's the Fourth of July, then Christmas again! I think I have an explanation for that phenomenon. Time is indeed relative for each of us and what we have experienced, not only in an Einsteinian way. A year to a one-year-old child is his or her entire lifetime.

As I write this, I am in my eightieth year since my birth on this earth; so a year is, to me, approximately 1.25 percent of my lifetime. I am about 4,210 weeks old as I am writing this paragraph, so one week is approximately 0.024 percent of my life so far. That is why it seems to go by so fast because there is so much time that has passed for each division of time to be relative to, and I really believe that is the reason time seems to speed up as we age. In fact, time has gone by so fast that as I have made some additions to clarify what I have written, I am now eighty-two.

I had planned to stop writing a long time ago, but it is hard to do because questions keep popping into my head! When I saw Bob that early morning when I went to support operations, did he also see me? If he saw me, did he see me as I appeared in the flesh at that time or as a ghost or other apparition? If he saw me, what was his reaction other than to disappear before I could see if he was still there, which of course I don't know if he was because I no longer saw him.

Maybe I could no longer see him because I knew he shouldn't be there because he was "dead." Myra obviously saw me because she was staring right at me when I "saw" her. Did she see me as clearly as I "saw" her? One day, I may have the answer to that, but maybe only after I become the same form of entity as she was.

Do we, as spirits, occupy only one universe at a time; or is part of us actually in another universe as well, where we gather psychic information? If we occupied more than one universe at a time, we would necessarily be of, or carry with us, different elements in each universe; and that could explain somewhat, when our individual psychic abilities kick in, the different apparitions each of us sees when we see a spirit.

21

Where and What Are We Really?

After the body dies, I have no doubt that we exist as an entity of some sort and we don't go anywhere. We simply go on "living," possibly in a different universe but still in the UNIVERSE of course and maybe still in this universe because I have seen some of us still looking very much alive right here with us even though I knew they are "dead."

We are here now, and we will still be "here" after we separate from our bodies. The change for us will be what being "here" means in whatever universe we then inhabit until we move on to a different universe or back to this one for another try at "life" here. The real us may consist of some sort of energy form or assembly of various energies. We may inhabit living assemblies of matter and energy in various universes within the UNIVERSE, or the many mansions as Jesus may have called them, depending on what our purpose or goal is in the particular universe we inhabit.

In the Bible, someone has written "God separated the waters from the dry land." Does that imply that the universe we live in was separated from the original primary UNIVERSE and does it imply that the UNIVERSE exists as something similar to our water and does that also imply that we (in our original form) have been some sort of aquatic beings, whatever aquatic means in other parts of the UNIVERSE?

People have reported seeing spirits floating in the air, so maybe they are really floating in whatever the "aquatic" medium of their universe is. It wouldn't be water (or we would all drown), but some other form of exotic energy or foreign substance that we live in as spirits. Or was that reference to waters only to earth? Did we live as some sort of matter (as we know life) or just exist in some form of substance or energy totally different from matter?

What are we doing in this limited universe instead of in a state in which we are capable of perceiving all there is? Maybe we, in our original spiritual form, actually helped create or evolve life in this universe, on this planet, and decided we wanted to experience life and accidently got trapped due to the overwhelming limitations life imposed on our being when we attempted to inhabit those life-forms.

I believe we may have helped the evolution of some of the species on this planet by influencing how they developed physically, making them more curious about where they lived, desire for certain foods, use of tools, and selection of mates; but most importantly, we implanted dreams and warnings of danger. Eventually, we helped evolve the human being as good or as bad as that may seem to be!

This is sort of what Edgar Cayce said happened: that we projected ourselves into matter and animals and got stuck, but he didn't say we helped create the life-forms here but did say human beings were developed to help us find our way back where we belong. For some reason, or maybe no reason, we created karma, whether or not it is necessary for our development.

We come back to fix things and only end up in the trap again because we don't remember why we are here and our bodies are more in control of what happens than our soul can influence what we do. Could this be what someone interpreted as being expelled from heaven because we are no longer capable of seeing heaven or experiencing it while we are here? Maybe the biblical apple we were not supposed to have is experiencing life as it exists here in this universe on this earth, or maybe some just instinctively think it is while we are in this state of being. Although I don't believe in it, some call it original sin.

Maybe God is the only real entity; and we, as a minute part of it, are given the responsibility of living life for its experience. There may be other forms of experience on other planets or in other "universes." If this is what we are, then God is experiencing some really weird stuff when he has been experiencing my life, and I imagine some other lives too.

If that is what is happening, the idea of a place called hell becomes more ridiculous because God would not put a part of itself in hell. Many of us are doing a lousy job of living God's life if that is the case. If we are living physical life in this universe for the experience of a supreme being that created this magnificent UNIVERSE and if we knew we were, how would we live our lives?

I think I would try to be constructive and have at least a little bit of fun (if I hadn't been so shy), but not at the expense of others who are also living a life for that being. Is the soul supposed to be in command of these bodies? If so, it's probably not doing a good job of it because there were people like Hitler, Stalin, and other murderous leaders in several countries plus mass murderers whose souls must have given up trying to keep them corralled and doing the right thing.

There are a lot of people who don't seem to care about doing anything right, take advantage of others every chance they get and seem to have no conscience. There are a lot of souls in state and federal governments right now who must be about ready to throw in the towel! I know mine is probably scratching its head (if it has one) and wondering how could all souls have totally lost control like this! This place has really gone over the edge, and there is only insane rain falling everywhere! But there is still hope hopefully.

I believe we are spiritual beings temporarily living a physical existence in time and space and sometimes not enjoying it much. I believe we, the real us, are already living an eternal life and don't have to earn the right to eternal life. This may be only a small part of what we have to experience; and we will probably experience much more in the future, speaking as though time exists for the real us and human beings may be around on this planet until our sun, Sol, turns into a red giant and fries this planet earth. But that won't happen for millions of years.

That brings up another fact that many of us ask the wrong question about. We question how many solar systems there are in our galaxy and the universe. There is one *solar* system named for one of the names of the star earth and the various other planets and asteroids revolve around. The other stars with planetary systems are really stellar systems. Maybe some have names, and maybe some do not. I believe there are many planets around many stars with life-forms on them that we, as spirits, may have helped evolve.

Where are we? Are we totally inside these bodies we inhabit or are we or a part of us still somehow separate from them? Is this body acting as an avatar to the soul? I know there has to be a connection to where we originated, but is it continuous or momentary as needed to get needed help occasionally?

I do believe that, as I said before, we have almost constant communication with others like us. I believe we are still in what we call heaven but cannot see it or experience it because we are where we are in this limited universe with its limited resources, its speed limit, the limited energy in it, and the limitations imposed by the bodies we occupy.

We may see only a limited additional part of it when we are in between lives that we must experience on this planet or maybe even other planets in this universe or in other universes if we need to or during expanded sense moments. As long as we depend on our eyes to see where we are, we will not see heaven because of the limitations imposed by this physical universe and the electromagnetic phenomena in it. When we have reached the goal, whatever that is, we will really experience heaven again.

I have generated many questions, and I think I have generated possible answers to some of them. Hopefully, some of the answers are right.

About the Author

Arthur (Art) Seter, born and raised on a farm in North Dakota, earned a bachelor of science degree in electrical engineering at the University of North Dakota. Employed in civil service by the U.S. Navy for thirty-nine years, he designed equipment used for the development testing of various aircraft and weapons including Harpoon antiship and Tomahawk cruise missiles.

His main hobby is amateur astronomy; but he also spends time reading, traveling in the U.S., and playing video games. He currently resides in Ventura California with his wife of fifty-four years and has two children and four grandchildren.